Hank Aaron

HOME RUN HERO

By Jessica Morrison

Crabtree Publishing Company
www.crabtreebooks.com

Crabtree Publishing Company

www.crabtreebooks.com

Author: Jessica Morrison
Publishing plan research and development:
  Sean Charlebois, Reagan Miller
  Crabtree Publishing Company
Editors: Mark Sachner, Lynn Peppas
Proofreader: Wendy Scavuzzo
Indexer: Wendy Scavuzzo
Editorial director: Kathy Middleton
Photo researcher: Ruth Owen
Designer: Alix Wood
Production coordinator: Margaret Amy Salter
Production: Kim Richardson
Prepress technician: Margaret Amy Salter

Written, developed, and produced by
Water Buffalo Books

Publisher's note:
All quotations in this book come from original sources and contain the spelling and grammatical inconsistencies of the original text. Some quotations may also contain terms that may be considered inappropriate or offensive. The use of such terms is for the sake of preserving the historical and literary accuracy of the sources and should not be seen as endorsing the use of such terms.

Photographs and reproductions:
Corbis: Bettmann Archive: page 41 (main); Bettmann Archive: page 65
Flickr Creative Commons: page 103
Getty Images: Dave Martin: page 15; National Baseball Hall of Fame: page 35; Rogers Photo Archive: page 39; Richard Meek: page 55; Transcendental Graphics: page 63; R. Bennett: page 79; Herb Scharfman: page 85
Public domain: front cover (main); page 4 (inset); page 30; page 31; page 33; page 37; page 38; page 45 (all); page 48 (right); page 67 (inset); page 73; page 74 (all); page 75 (all); page 77 (inset); page 86 (right); page 93 (inset)
Shutterstock: front cover (background); page 4 (background); page 7 (background right); page 8; page 9 (background); page 12; page 13; page 14; pages 16-17; page 22; page 23; page 24; page 25; page 32; page 36; page 40; page 41 (right); page 42; page 43; page 48 (left); page 52; page 56; page 57; page 58; page 60; page 61; page 62; page 66; page 67 (background); page 68; page 69 (background); page 72; page 76; page 77 (background); page 82; page 83; page 84; page 85 (background); page 86 (left); page 92; page 93 (background); page 96; page 98; page 99; page 101; page 102
Water Buffalo Books: page 1; page 7 (top); page 46; page 47; page 53; page 69 (left); page 95 (top); page 97
Wikipedia (public domain): page 5; page 7 (bottom); page 9 (main); page 11; page 15 (bottom); page 21; page 29; page 49; page 51; page 71; page 89; page 91; page 95 (bottom)

Cover: When 18-year-old Hank Aaron first stepped onto the train in Mobile that would to take him to his dreams, he had no idea how his life would turn out. His career in baseball spanned the generation that saw the United States move from segregation, through the civil rights movement, to an era of greater understanding. Revered by fans and reviled by bigots, Hank Aaron was determined to leave a legacy that was more than just "Baseball's Greatest Hitter."

Library and Archives Canada Cataloguing in Publication	Library of Congress Cataloging-in-Publication Data

Morrison, J. A. (Jessica A.), 1984-
  Hank Aaron : home run hero / Jessica Morrison.
 	
(Crabtree groundbreaker biographies)
Includes index.
Issued also in an electronic format.
ISBN 978-0-7787-2538-1 (bound).--ISBN 978-0-7787-2547-3 (pbk.)
 	
  1. Aaron, Hank, 1934- --Juvenile literature. 2. Baseball players--United States--Biography--Juvenile literature. 3. African American baseball players--Biography--Juvenile literature.
I. Title. II. Series: Crabtree groundbreaker biographies
 	
GV865.A25M67 2011   j796.357092   C2010-903034-6
	Morrison, Jessica.
	  Hank Aaron : home run hero / Jessica Morrison.
	    p. cm. -- (Crabtree groundbreaker biographies)
	  Includes index.
	  ISBN 978-0-7787-2547-3 (pbk. : alk. paper) --
	ISBN 978-0-7787-2538-1 (reinforced library binding : alk. paper) -- ISBN 978-1-4271-9470-1 (electronic (pdf))
	  1. Aaron, Hank, 1934---Juvenile literature. 2. Baseball players--United States--Biography--Juvenile literature. 3. African American baseball players--Biography--Juvenile literature. I. Title. II. Series.
	
	GV865.A25M665 2011
	796.357092--dc22
	[B]
	
	                      2010018111

Crabtree Publishing Company

www.crabtreebooks.com   1-800-387-7650

Printed in the USA/082010/BL20100723

Published in Canada
Crabtree Publishing
616 Welland Ave.
St. Catharines, Ontario
L2M 5V6

Published in the United States
Crabtree Publishing
PMB 59051
350 Fifth Avenue, 59th Floor
New York, New York 10118

Published in the United Kingdom
Crabtree Publishing
Maritime House
Basin Road North, Hove
BN41 1WR

Published in Australia
Crabtree Publishing
386 Mt. Alexander Rd.
Ascot Vale (Melbourne)
VIC 3032

Contents

hank aaron

MILWAUKEE BRAVES
OUTFIELD

Chapter 1
Two Homers, Two Moments in History

On September 23, 1957, young Henry (Hank) Aaron stepped up to the plate with two outs in the bottom of the 11th. Focusing on the ball in Cardinal pitcher Billy Muffett's hand, Hank ignored the screaming

Eventually, Hank became the major-league all-time leader in home runs.

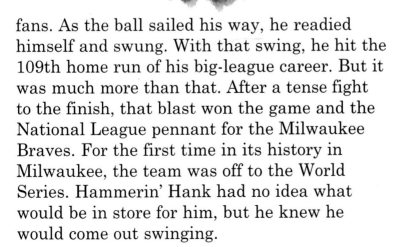

fans. As the ball sailed his way, he readied himself and swung. With that swing, he hit the 109th home run of his big-league career. But it was much more than that. After a tense fight to the finish, that blast won the game and the National League pennant for the Milwaukee Braves. For the first time in its history in Milwaukee, the team was off to the World Series. Hammerin' Hank had no idea what would be in store for him, but he knew he would come out swinging.

Opposite: Hank Aaron's 1958 baseball card.

THE COLOR LINE

Major League Baseball has never had an official policy banning African-Americans. But nearly all of organized baseball (the major leagues and their minor-league affiliates) had an "unwritten" rule excluding black players from the late 1800s through 1946. That was the year that the Brooklyn Dodgers signed Jackie Robinson. The terms "color line" and "color barrier," which apply to any exclusion of people on the basis of race, have become a part of the sport's historic record—and its vocabulary.

Troubled Times

That same day, a group of African-American children tried without success to enter all-white Little Rock Central High School in Little Rock, Arkansas. These nine students simply wanted an education, but they were refused at the door. The next day, they would be escorted by U.S. National Guard troops ordered into Little Rock by the U.S. government. These armed escorts were needed to protect the kids from violence at the hands of an angry mob of white people who were determined to keep black kids out of all-white Little Rock Central.

The Toast of the Town

Aaron would win the 1957 National League Most Valuable Player award, and the Braves went on to defeat the American League's New York Yankees in a thrilling seven-game World Series. Eventually, Hank became the major-league all-time leader in home runs (755), runs batted in (2,297), extra-base hits (1,477), and total bases (6,856). That day, however, ten years after Jackie Robinson had broken the color line in big-league baseball with the Brooklyn Dodgers, Henry Aaron was carried off the field by his ecstatic teammates, white and black alike. At the same time that Little Rock was erupting in racial hatred, Hank Aaron became the toast of Milwaukee.

Some Hard Truths

Sixteen years later, the Braves had moved from Milwaukee to Atlanta. Hank Aaron was still hitting home runs—a lot of them—now for the

Hank Aaron counts the home run he hit on September 23, 1957, to give the Braves their first pennant in Milwaukee, as the most prized of the 755 he hit during his legendary career. He later described being carried off the field by his

teammates (including Eddie Mathews and Warren Spahn, shown with Hank above) as "my shiningest hour." He told of the moment as one that would remain forever frozen in time for him: "I can't tell you who was carrying me because you know something? I don't remember that at all. But I remember looking up at the clock and seeing 11:34."

TWO MOMENTS FROZEN IN TIME

During that same 24-hour period, another moment became frozen in time. That moment was captured by a photo that would become a symbol of racial hatred in the United States at the dawn of the civil rights era. At that moment, Elizabeth Eckford found herself dropped off a block away from Little Rock (Arkansas) Central High School. Cut off from the other African-American students in her group, Elizabeth endured the taunts and threats screamed at her by the all-white crowd around her (below) as she calmly and purposefully walked to school with her head held high.

Atlanta Braves. Unlike Milwaukee in 1957, Atlanta in 1973 was a place where baseball's segregationist past was more in evidence than in the North. As he approached Babe Ruth's all-time record of 714 homers, it was Hank, not high school kids, who needed an armed bodyguard this time.

Throughout most of the 1973 season, Hank received thousands of letters a day. Most of the mail he received consisted of hate mail, some of it (like that shown on the page opposite), containing death threats against him and members of his family. Hank spent most of that season cut off from his teammates, surrounded by bodyguards, unable to bask in the glory of his assault on the home run record. Despite all this, Hank finished the 1973 season with a .301 batting average, 96 RBIs (runs batted in), and 40 homers—leaving him one short of tying Ruth.

Beating the Babe

On the opening day of the 1974 season, Hank Aaron hit home run number 714 to tie the Babe's home run record. It had been a long and draining road, and he had almost become accustomed to the hate mail that was piling up. As Hank said,

"There's no way to measure the effect that those letters had on me, but I like to think that every one ... added another home run to my total."

Just a few days later, on April 8, 1974, Hank socked number 715. He knew he would never have another moment like it. But he also knew his work, and his legacy, were just beginning.

"Everybody loved Babe Ruth. You will be the most hated man in this country if you break his career home run record."

***

"You black animal, I hope you never live long enough to hit more home runs than the great Babe Ruth."

"Dear Hank, ...if you come close to Babe Ruth's 714 homers I have a contract out on you.... If by the all-star game you have come within 20 homers of babe you will be shot on sight by one of my assassins..."

Anonymous hate mail sent to Hank Aaron during his drive to break Babe Ruth's all-time home run record

Hank watches number 715 head for the stands.

Chapter 2
Big Dreams in A Small Town

On February 5, 1934, Henry (Hank) Aaron entered the world in Mobile, Alabama. At the time, home run king Babe Ruth was one day shy of his 39th birthday. The Babe, bed-ridden with a case of influenza, had no idea his successor had been born just 1,000 miles (1,600 km) south.

Segregation: A Part of Daily Life

Although the South had long been a stronghold of racial segregation, Mobile was known for being relatively ahead of its time in progress regarding race relations. Two decades before Hank's birth, John LeFlore, an African-American postal worker, had a fight with a white man trying to keep him off the bus. Later, he formed the Mobile chapter of the National Association for the Advancement of Colored People (NAACP). Unlike most other

Hank would throw the ball on the roof and run around the house, catching it as it fell off the other side.

parts of the South, the Mobile public library was available to both white and black people, and the private college was integrated. Even with these small advancements, segregation was still a part of daily life for the Aarons.

... [N]obody could have guessed he was on his way to becoming a baseball legend.

Hank was his parents' third child and would later become one of eight children in the Aaron household. His father, Herbert, worked at a shipbuilding dock. His mother, Estella, stayed home with the children and occasionally cleaned houses for two dollars each. Thoughts of baseball were far from everyone's mind, yet young Hank was taken with the simple game of ball, stick, and glove. By the age of four, he was hooked. Since times were tough, Hank practiced hitting bottle caps with a stick, and his father gave him homemade baseballs made of golf balls wrapped in nylon stockings. Hank would throw the ball on the roof and run around the house, catching it as it fell off the other side. It was great practice, but nobody could have guessed he was on his way to becoming a baseball legend.

After their sixth child, Herbert decided to move his family to Toulminville. This was a small village outside the city limits, with less hustle and bustle and more room for his growing family. They bought two oversized lots and built their own six-bedroom home. It was twice the house they were used to, and they patched it up as extra money came in. It was a full household, but it was full of love and pride.

There was no running water or electricity in the new house, but the Aarons were proud to have a place of their own. They fetched water from a well and gathered wood to heat the house. With so many mouths to feed, the staples were butter beans, cornbread, and collard greens. Hank used to call his sister "Neck Bone" because she was so skinny. "We all described ourselves as six o'clock—straight up and down," he recalled. Years later, when Hank wore number 44, a team official told him he was too skinny for such a big number.

A Great Place for Baseball

Toulminville gave Hank great opportunities for pursuing his love for baseball. He remembers there was "no better place to play ball than Toulminville." Unlike Mobile, Toulminville had wide open spaces for playing. He and his friends played pickup games in a vacant lot near his home. They created their own baseball diamond in a pecan grove and were soon playing every day after school and whenever they could get out of chores.

A few years later, when Toulminville became part of Mobile, Carver Park was built on the same site. This became the first officially designated recreational spot for African-Americans in Mobile.

Hank's all-black elementary school didn't have a baseball team, but he and his friends had their own diamond in the grove. It soon became one of Hank's favorite places.

Organized team or not, Hank and his buddies played a really good brand of baseball. In fact, a lot of great ball players came from Toulminville. Along with Hank, Satchel Paige, Willie McCovey, and Billy Williams were raised there. Eventually, all four became enshrined in the Baseball Hall of Fame. Although white players also came out of Toulminville and joined the major leagues, Hank and his friends couldn't play with them as youngsters. In fact,

Although softball was big in Hank's community, he really only saw it as something to do until he could play baseball. For Hank, life was all about baseball from the start.

as Hank later recalled, most black people "didn't know any white people unless they worked for them."

Hank played for the school's fast-pitch softball team because his school didn't have a baseball team. He pitched and played catcher and several infield positions. He also hit quite a few home runs. His team was called the Braves, named after the big-league Braves who, at the time, played in Boston. Although softball was big in Hank's community, he really

Above: Hank Aaron (right) addresses fans during ceremonies opening a museum in his childhood home on April 14, 2010, in Mobile, Alabama. The museum stands near Hank Aaron Stadium (above, background, and below, as shown at night), home of the Mobile Baybears of the Southern League.

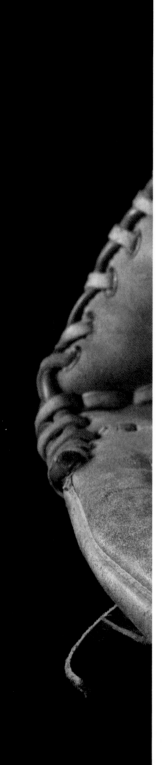

only saw it as something to do until he could play baseball. For Hank, life was all about baseball from the start.

On the field, Hank had talent that was apparent to all. But he also stood out because of a few unusual habits. When he eventually played big-league ball, one of his teammates called him "Snowshoes" because of how he ran on his heels. Hank also had an unusual batting stance. He placed his front foot, his left, farther forward and put more weight on it than was usual. This may have been to compensate for an injury.

This stance may also have led to a view of him as gripping the bat "cross-handed," with his left hand on top instead of his right. According to Ed Scott, who "discovered" Hank playing sandlot ball in Mobile and became his manager on a local black team:

> "I never once saw him hit cross-handed. I know because I've seen guys who hit cross-handed and he didn't ... [T]hat was something I missed, something I know for a fact I would have noticed. I'm telling you, I never saw it, but that became part of the legend. No point arguing about it now."

Hank recalled his strange manner of running "got [me] around the bases in pretty good fashion" and felt that his batting stance and swing were just fine. He watched the Mobile Bears playing at nearby Hartwell Field and noticed nobody batted like him, but he was still hitting homers and saw no reason to change.

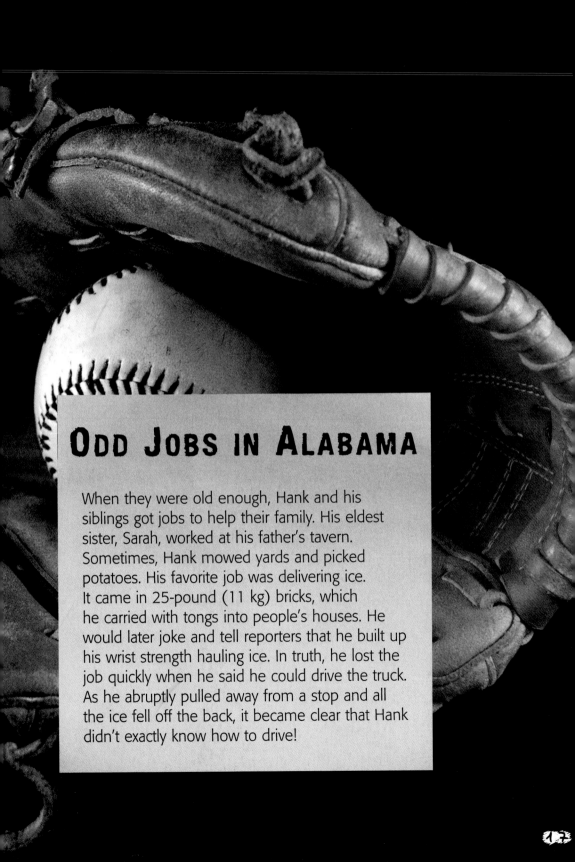

Odd Jobs in Alabama

When they were old enough, Hank and his siblings got jobs to help their family. His eldest sister, Sarah, worked at his father's tavern. Sometimes, Hank mowed yards and picked potatoes. His favorite job was delivering ice. It came in 25-pound (11 kg) bricks, which he carried with tongs into people's houses. He would later joke and tell reporters that he built up his wrist strength hauling ice. In truth, he lost the job quickly when he said he could drive the truck. As he abruptly pulled away from a stop and all the ice fell off the back, it became clear that Hank didn't exactly know how to drive!

Jackie Opens the Door

Although Hank showed obvious talent on the field, not everybody wanted him to pursue professional ball. Until 1947, when Jackie Robinson broke baseball's color line by playing with the Brooklyn Dodgers, Hank's father told him, "Ain't no colored ball players." His mother saw baseball as something that would just get in the way of his education. If Hank was to play any sports, she wished it would be football because she thought he could get a college scholarship. Although he played briefly for his high school football team, Hank quit after a few days. Colleges didn't offer scholarships to baseball players, but Hank had his mind set. He wanted to focus completely on baseball.

In 1947, his dream grew bigger when Robinson became not only a Dodger, but the first African-American to join the modern major leagues. Breaking the color line, Jackie became a hero to Hank and his friends. He even skipped school to hear Jackie speak in the auditorium near his home in 1948. It was that day that Hank vowed to his father that he would be in the big leagues before Jackie retired. Hank remembered feeling so inspired by Jackie, feeling that "he breathed baseball into the black community." In fact, Hank was so driven to play ball that he didn't keep up in school—that was ironic, as Jackie had preached the importance of kids staying in school on the day Hank heard him.

At one point, Hank skipped 40 days of school in a row to hang out at a local pool hall—not to play pool but to listen to Dodger games on the radio. Hank was suspended, but by then he didn't put much stock in school anyway.

Hank was afraid to tell his parents he was suspended, but his dad soon figured it out. One afternoon, Herbert marched into the pool hall and told Hank to follow him out. After a long talk in the car, Hank's father made him promise to return to school for his education. He also told Hank that he would be attending an all-black private school, the Josephine Allen Institute, in the fall.

Hank began playing shortstop for the Black Bears every Sunday. As a teenager among men, he looked skinny and awkward. But once he picked up a bat, people knew why he was there.

Hank didn't have to worry about school until the coming fall, so he spent his time earning a bit of money and playing ball. Soon, manager Ed Scott of the Mobile Black Bears, a small, independent Negro League team, noticed Hank playing. Scott offered Hank a spot on his team.

Hank knew the offer would upset his mother. The Black Bears were grown men, and they played on Sundays. He knew that as a devout, church-going woman, his mother wouldn't approve of playing on a day normally spent on family and worship. Hank didn't have a hope of

JACKIE ROBINSON:
THE MAN AND HIS LEGACY

In 1946, Branch Rickey, the owner of the Brooklyn Dodgers, decided to make a bold move. In what became known as "baseball's great experiment," Rickey spoke to Jackie about the possibility of joining the Dodgers, thereby becoming the first African-American to play Major League Baseball. He wanted to know if Jackie would be able to handle the abuse that would come his way, including hate letters, threats of violence, and prejudice on and off the field. For this "experiment" in integrating baseball to succeed, Rickey needed a man "with enough guts to not fight back." After a lengthy talk, Jackie agreed and signed on with the Montreal Royals, the Dodgers' farm team.

The announcement that a black man was joining a big-league organization caused a sensation, particularly in heavily segregated Florida, where the teams held spring training. Local officials canceled games in which the Dodgers were playing and, as Rickey had predicted, Jackie endured prejudice every day. But he quietly and diplomatically continued to play the game to the best of his ability. After a tremendous season in Montreal, he was called up to the Dodgers for the 1947 season.

Although he received a mixed reception by other players, especially those on opposing teams, African-American fans flocked to support him. His strength of character helped him play through the trials of the season. He won the Rookie of the Year award that year and, two years later, in 1949, he won the National League Most Valuable Player award.

Jackie Robinson is now known as one of the most influential players in the history of baseball. At the time he was called up to the Dodgers, the Supreme Court was still seven years away from ruling segregation in schools as unconstitutional. It was a time when standing up for racial equality was typically met by violence and hatred. By facing discrimination and exercising self-control, he paved the way for other African-American players.

Later in 1947, Larry Doby integrated the American League when he appeared with the Cleveland Indians and, by 1948, a number of other African-American players joined the big leagues. By then, the Dodgers alone had signed three more black players. Like other players inspired by Jackie's integrity, Hank Aaron credits much of his success to Jackie's presence in the sport.

Jackie Robinson is shown in 1950 holding the National League Most Valuable Player award that he won for his performance in the 1949 season.

convincing his mother, so he avoided Ed Scott as best he could. Often, Hank would hide as soon as he saw Ed approach.

Scott was persistent. At one point, he visited Hank's house every weekend and spoke to Mrs. Aaron. After a month of relentless visits, she finally gave in, and Hank officially joined the team. There were conditions on his parents' giving him permission to play. For one thing, he was only allowed to play in home games and had to return to school in the fall. Ed also assured Mrs. Aaron that Hank would be making ten dollars a game ($84 by today's standards). For a teenager in 1950, this was a sum of which Hank could be quite proud.

Hank began playing shortstop for the Black Bears every Sunday. As a teenager among men, he looked skinny and awkward. But once he picked up a bat, people knew why he was there. Ed Scott remembered:

> *"He was green as he could be ... the other team figured he wasn't ready. The pitcher tried to get a fastball by him, and he hit a line drive that banged against the old tin fence.... [He] nearly put the ball through the fence."*

On that day, nobody could have known just how far that swing would take Hank.

Downs and the Clowns

In the fall of 1950, Hank made good on his promise to his mother and started attending the Josephine Allen Institute. Baseball was never far from his mind, but he did his best during school hours.

In spring 1951, Hank continued playing with the Black Bears. At the time, playing with the Bears was about the best Hank could hope for but, his manager, Ed Scott, had other plans for him. Scott was also a scout for the Indianapolis Clowns of the Negro American League. He got in touch with McKinley "Bunny" Downs, the business manager of the Clowns, telling Downs to come by for the day and watch Hank play.

With Downs watching from the stands, Hank put on quite a show on the field, collecting three base hits and showing good range at

One day, Hank opened his mailbox to find a contract offering him $200 a month to play for the Indianapolis Clowns. He was ecstatic!

shortstop. After the game, Downs approached Hank and asked if he would like to play for the Clowns. Playing for the Clowns would be a huge step up in Negro League play but, once again, Hank knew his mother wouldn't go for it. Like Ed Scott, however, Bunny Downs was persistent. He arranged to meet with Mrs. Aaron and told her that they could send for Hank once he was finished with high school. Hank had just turned 17.

The following months at school were difficult for Hank. While he was trying to concentrate

on school, every time he heard a game on the radio, he began to fantasize that he was playing the big leagues. He was also worried that he had missed his shot at professional ball. Every day he checked his mailbox, eager to find the contract Downs had promised. By winter, Hank had almost given up on this step in achieving his big-league dreams.

Then, one day, Hank opened his mailbox to find a contract offering him $200 a month to play for the Indianapolis Clowns. He was ecstatic! He was to meet the team for spring training in Winston-Salem, North Carolina. To get to North Carolina, Hank would take the trip of his life. Soon after receiving the

Ball players were traditionally hard on rookies, but the Clowns were especially rough on Hank.

contract, he would be on a train chugging away from Mobile, his mother, and everything he knew—and he was scared. "I guess I had good reason to be scared," he recalled, "All I had going for me was my bat, and I didn't even know how to hold it right."

Spring Training

In May 1952, Hank boarded the train for North Carolina with two sandwiches, two clean pairs of pants, and two dollars. He also had with him an envelope that he was to give to Downs, from Ed Scott, his old manager with the Black Bears. Hank's mother had been so upset as he left, she couldn't even see him off at the train station. Hank watched from the train window as his father, siblings, and manager grew small in the distance as the train chugged away.

Hank was more than a little nervous. With his knees knocking together, he wondered if he had done the right thing by leaving Alabama. He tried to talk himself out of getting off at the next stop and going home. What if he couldn't impress the Clowns once he'd arrived? What if they sent him home humiliated?

He never did look inside the envelope he was carrying, but he later found out what Scott had written to Downs: "Forget everything else about this player. Just watch his bat."

When he arrived at the Clowns' training camp, Hank wasn't received well by the other players. New players joining the team normally meant than an older player would be cut. Plus, as a quiet kid who knew little about the world, Hank was also an easy target.

Knowing that young Hank would get a chance at the majors they never would, the older players taunted him relentlessly. They made fun of his worn-out shoes and asked if he got his glove at the Salvation Army. Ball players were traditionally hard on rookies, but the Clowns were especially rough on Hank. Nearly every day, he was the butt of some sort of joke.

Trying to stay positive, Hank focused on his game. True to their name, the Clowns often did funny things on the field. They would play

imaginary games of catch, or the catcher sometimes sat behind the plate in a rocking chair. They even flew buckets of confetti at the crowd. The fans loved every minute.

The Clowns were also the best team in the league, and they played a tough schedule. Playing as many as ten games a week in many towns, Hank learned how to sleep on a bus full of players. To make matters worse, the team slept on the bus every night except Saturdays, when they stayed in a hotel.

People soon began to notice the scrawny kid from Toulminville. Hank was hitting .400 and batting fourth in the lineup. Helping the Clowns win game after game, he was even starting to make headlines. His first taste of publicity came when the *Pittsburgh Courier* wrote about his batting and fielding, calling him a "shining light."

The Clowns' owner, Syd Pollack, knew he had a good player in Hank. He also knew he had serious money-making potential. Hank didn't realize it, but several major-league teams had put scouts on his trail. Scouts had even begun calling his family's home in Mobile.

Pollack wrote to John Mullen, the minor-league director of the Boston Braves. Interested in finding out what all the Aaron fuss was about, Mullen sent scout Dewey Griggs to watch him play.

The Clowns were playing a doubleheader in Buffalo, New York. After watching Hank throughout the first game, Griggs introduced himself and told him he had concerns about his playing, particularly his running and his batting stance. Hank normally ran at three-quarter speed because his father told him to never hurry unless he had to. Despite this, Griggs had this to say in his report back to Director Mullen: "This boy could be the answer."

About a month later, Griggs returned to watch Hank play again. He wanted to make sure he was a consistent player and not a one-hit wonder. Hank tallied up seven hits, including two home runs, in nine at bats. It looked as if Hank was extremely consistent.

Suddenly, Hank was a wanted man. The Dodgers, who had rejected him in an earlier tryout in 1949, became interested. The Braves and the Dodgers started a bidding war. Not to miss out on the rising star, the New York Giants also joined in the battle over Hank.

Hank was overwhelmed. The Braves were offering him $350 a month and would probably send him to Wisconsin to play for their Class-C minor-league farm team, the Eau Claire Bears, in the Northern League. The Giants offered to pay him $300 a month to play for their farm team in the Interstate League. Ultimately, Hank chose the Braves. Hank has said that his choice had mostly to do with the money and the fairness of the Braves' offer, but he has also said that he'd noticed the Giants misspelled his name as "Arron" on their telegram!

Because he was still a minor, Hank's father had to sign the contract as well. Before signing, however, Herbert took it straight to a lawyer to be inspected. During his final two weeks with the Clowns, Hank continued to lead the league in hitting. When it came time to leave, everyone, including Hank, was anxious to see how he would fare with the Braves.

"I had the Giants' contract in my hand. But the Braves offered 50 dollars a month more. That's the only thing that kept Willie Mays and me from being teammates— 50 dollars."

Hank Aaron

Chapter 3
Movin' On Up

Hank knew that he needed to prove himself in the minor leagues before he could make it up to the parent club in the majors. Getting to join his new team in Eau Claire, Wisconsin, meant flying, and Hank had never been in a plane before. He was a bundle of nerves in the two-engine commuter plane, where he felt bounces and heard sounds that a more experienced air traveler would probably have ignored. On top of his nervousness over flying, Hank had plenty of time to become more and more aware that, once again, he was heading off into unknown territory.

A New Life on and off the Field

Hank showed up in central Wisconsin in the middle of the 1952 season and joined his new team, the Eau Claire Bears, when they returned from a road trip. Hank learned that there were only two other African-American players on the team—catcher Julie Bowers and

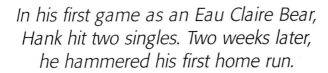

In his first game as an Eau Claire Bear, Hank hit two singles. Two weeks later, he hammered his first home run.

outfielder Wes Covington. This was the first time Hank would be playing on an integrated team, and he was very intimidated. "There was nothing in my experience that prepared me for white people," he later wrote. His worries about playing on a mostly white team were made even worse by his fear that he might not be as talented as his teammates and that he would be judged harshly.

By the end of his first minor-league season, he had the league's second-highest batting average. He was also named Rookie of the Year.

Hank soon learned that he needn't have been scared. As he later recalled,

> *"When you hear all your life that you're inferior, it makes you wonder if the other guys have something you've never seen before. It didn't take long to find out that the ball was still round after it left a white pitcher's hand, and it responded the same way when you hit it with a bat."*

In his first game as an Eau Claire Bear, Hank hit two singles. Two weeks later, he hammered his first home run.

He was a success on the field, but he came to find that his off-the-field life was a different

story. He missed his family and was terribly lonely and homesick. Although the North wasn't as racially charged as the South, Hank still felt that he didn't blend in with the small-town community. People often stared at him in restaurants, and he became quiet and shy. He had never been talkative to begin with, but now he retreated into silence more than ever.

Feeling alone and isolated, Hank packed his cardboard suitcase and called his family to tell them he was returning home. Luckily, his brother Herbert Jr. took the phone when Hank called. He said that if Hank left, he'd be walking out on the best break he could hope for and that he'd be crazy to leave. Deciding his brother was right, Hank chose to stay and play ball no matter how difficult it was.

Hank was lucky his brother had given him a pep talk. In mid-July he was picked to play in the Northern League All-Star game, as a shortstop. By the end of his first minor-league season, he had the league's second-highest batting average. He was also named Rookie of the Year. With a batting average of .336 and nine home runs and 61 RBIs in 87 games, Hank was already on his way to becoming a baseball star.

The Negro League World Series

When the Northern League's season ended, Hank returned to play with the Indianapolis Clowns. The team was playing in the Negro League World Series. He helped the Clowns win the series in a best-of-13-game marathon that was played all over the South. One of their games brought the Clowns to Mobile. It was the first time Hank had been home since he had left in the spring, and he was welcomed with open arms. He was honored by a local service organization and even given a "Henry Aaron Day" at Hartwell Field. This honor struck Hank as somewhat ironic, since Hartwell Field was home to the Mobile Bears, a minor-league team that Hank would never have been able to play on before the Jackie Robinson era.

During the Clowns' 1952 season, Hank batted over .400 and hit five home runs. Although the local newspaper didn't report it, the Clowns went on to win the Negro League World Series. When the Series was over, he kept his promise to his mom to come home and finish high school.

The Color Line: Still in Play

Hank was moving up in the world of baseball. In 1953, he was assigned to the Jacksonville Braves, the Braves' Class A team in Florida. Being assigned to Jacksonville meant an even bigger change for Hank. Jacksonville was a previously all-white team in the South Atlantic League, better known as the Sally League. Hank would be one of the first African-Americans to desegregate the league—and the Deep South.

So That's What They See in This Guy

Rueben Stohs was a left-handed pitcher for Fargo-Moorhead in the Northern League. Stohs would one day become a renowned sports psychologist, but one of his most vivid sports moments was his first pitch to Hank. When Stohs first laid eyes on him, he wondered what the rest of the world saw in him:

> "He wasn't impressive physically, and his strike zone was from his shoes to the tip of his cap.... [T]he quickness of his bat was amazing. When I pitched to him that night, I got him out on a curve the first time. In the tenth inning the count went to three-and-two and I threw a high fastball. I could see his eyes get wide. He went up on his toes to get that ball, and just whipped it out of the park."

As a young player just up from the minors, Hank did not look like a typical power hitter. Opposing pitchers soon learned, however, that his ability to hit the long ball came from his patience at the plate, his good eye, and his quick wrists.

THE NEGRO LEAGUES—THE SHAME AND PRIDE OF BASEBALL

Before Jackie Robinson, Larry Doby, and others broke baseball's color line, African-American players were not allowed to play in any major or minor leagues that were affiliated with Major League Baseball. To combat this inequality, many black players formed their own leagues and teams and held their own games. These became known as the Negro Leagues.

The Negro Leagues have their roots in the late 19th and early 20th centuries. In the Midwest, there were the Chicago American Giants, Kansas City Monarchs, and Indianapolis ABCs, among others. In the East, the Cuban Stars and Homestead Grays became fan favorites. In the South, the Nashville Giants and Birmingham Black Bears established themselves as solid teams. African-American ballplayers looking for professional opportunities came out in droves, as did their fans to support them.

The Negro Leagues quickly became known for their talent. On one team alone—the Pittsburgh Crawfords—there were five future Baseball Hall of Famers (Satchel Paige, Cool Papa Bell, Josh Gibson, Judy Johnson, and Oscar Charleston). With talent that rivaled that of the all-white major-league teams throughout the country, the Negro Leagues soon became a popular attraction and favorite pastime of fans looking for great baseball.

In 1947, when Jackie Robinson broke the color line with the Dodgers, the Negro Leagues began to falter. Jackie Robinson had opened the doors to the major leagues, so many black players of the Negro Leagues went to join him. By 1952, most of the young talent in the Negro Leagues was signed into the majors. This resulted in a steady decline in attendance at Negro League games, and the teams' owners soon were met with financial trouble. After the 1949 season, the Negro League disintegrated. As the main talent moved on, the Negro Leagues were left behind.

Many Negro Leaguers, including Hank Aaron, later became inducted into the Baseball Hall of Fame after playing out spectacular careers in the American or National Leagues. Their beginnings in the Negro Leagues not only represent a piece of baseball history, but demonstrate the social development of the entire country. Today, the Negro Leagues are accorded respect and a stature that was not recognized or realized during their lifetime.

Champions Negro National League
1935

The 1935 Pittsburgh Crawfords of the Negro
National League pose for a team photo in front
of their bus. Many consider the Crawfords to be
the greatest black baseball team of all time. The
team included such legendary players as Josh
Gibson, Oscar Charleston, Cool Papa Bell, Judy
Johnson, and Leroy "Satchel" Paige.

Although Jackie Robinson had broken the color line in all of baseball, the major leagues at the time consisted entirely of teams that played in northern states. In the South, where many minor league teams were based, was a different story. The Sally League was firmly rooted in the segregationist culture of the states in which its teams played. In Louisiana, Georgia, Alabama, northern Florida, and South Carolina, it was virtually unthinkable for whites and blacks to play on the same team.

According to Hank in his autobiography, *I Had a Hammer*, even when teams added African-American players to a roster, local business groups and politicians would resist. In an example that reflects the bizarre logic of that time and place, one Florida business group, objecting to the local team's intention to field an integrated team, said that "No race prejudice is involved. It's just that the patrons of the team felt they would rather have an all-white team."

In the Deep South, it was scandalous and dangerous for any team to put a black man up to bat. When the Milwaukee Braves sent Hank Aaron, Félix Mantilla, and Horace Garner to Jacksonville, history was in the making.

Spectators and members of other teams shouted racist insults and dared Aaron, Mantilla, and Garner to lose their cool or perform badly.

hank aaron

MILWAUKEE BRAVES
OUTFIELD

*Hank Aaron's 1958 baseball card
included stats from the 1957 season,
in which he won the National
League Most Valuable Player
award. That year, he also helped
propel the Braves into the World
Series and past the Yankees,
whom they beat in seven games.
As suggested by the autograph
reprinted on this card, Aaron grew
up known as Henry, a name he
preferred to Hank.*

When Hank spent the 1953 season with the Braves' farm club in Jacksonville, he made history by helping break the color line in the South Atlantic League, which was then known as the Sally League.

To play with the Braves, Hank had to switch positions. Félix Mantilla was a skilled shortstop from Puerto Rico, so Hank became a second baseman instead. He didn't mind the switch and hit the team's only home run in their first game, but Hank and his African-American teammates had a tough time that year. The Deep South was one of the most racially sensitive areas of the nation, and they were playing smack dab in the middle of it.

Jacksonville's manager, Ben Geraghty, knew that the three young men would be hit hard. He sat down with Hank, Félix, and Horace and laid it all on the table. He told them that he would love to have them on his team. He also made it clear that they would be up against a lot, breaking the color line in the South. It meant a lot to Hank to hear these words. Although it didn't change how the rest of the world saw him, Hank was reassured to know his manager was on his side. "I never had a manager who cared more for his players or knew more about the game," he remembered.

His new manager was right. Every day brought new insults. Spectators and members of other teams shouted racist insults and dared Aaron, Mantilla, and Garner to lose their cool or perform badly. Pitchers even purposely tried to hit them with the ball, something that the three players never dignified with a reaction. "We knew that we not only had to play well, but if we ever lost our cool or caused an incident, it might set the whole program back five or ten years," Hank recalled.

It wasn't much different off the field. Just as Hank had to get used to Jacksonville, that city

This photo identified only the group of smiling Milwaukee Braves players—(left to right) Hank Aaron, Charlie White, and Bill Bruton—being served breakfast in 1954, which was Hank's first season in the majors. This probably took place during spring training in Florida, where black ball players who were refused service at hotels often had to stay with local families.

had to get used to him. Experiencing life as a second-class citizen was tough. When the team went out to eat at a restaurant, the black players were forced to eat in the restaurant kitchen. If they weren't allowed in the kitchen, their teammates would bring them food while they waited on the bus. Whenever the rest of the team stayed at a hotel, they were forced to stay in homes on the black side of town. To make them feel included, their manager always made a point to visit them in their rooms to make sure they were comfortable.

Despite the constant weight on his shoulders from racial tension, Hank was proving himself on the field. His 1953 season was a record breaker. He topped the league with a .362 batting average, 125 runs batted in (RBIs), 115 runs scored, 208 base hits, 338 total bases, and 36 doubles. He finished second in home runs, with 22. He was also honored as the league's Most Valuable Player and earned a spot on the Sally League All-Star team. The only problem Hank was noticing was his position. He felt he was a terrible second baseman. At the time, he thought, "we all knew that my best position was some other position."

Love and Marriage
Hank's life was also beginning to change in other ways. One day in 1953, he noticed a young woman walking into a post office. He was still at the ballpark, but he soon asked the team's clubhouse man, T.C. Marlin, who she

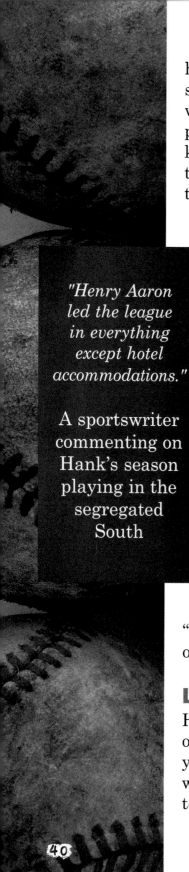

"Henry Aaron led the league in everything except hotel accommodations."

A sportswriter commenting on Hank's season playing in the segregated South

During the 1953 season at Jacksonville, Hank met, dated, fell in love with, and married a young student named Barbara Lucas. This photo is of the couple with their son Henry Jr. It was taken in 1957 at their home in Milwaukee during the time between Hank's pennant-winning home run against the St. Louis Cardinals and the Braves' World Series triumph against the New York Yankees.

was. Her name was Barbara Lucas, and she was attending classes at the local business college. Hank was immediately taken with her and asked her on a date. Later that year, they were married and Hank introduced Barbara to his family as his wife. The two were expecting their first child in 1954.

A Big Break

Following the 1953 season, Hank played winter ball in Puerto Rico. There, he was moved from second base to the outfield. When he reported for spring training in Bradenton, he hoped that he would be promoted to the parent club, but it soon became clear that the outfield was already full of experienced players. With guys like Jim Pendleton, Bill Bruton, Andy Pafko, and Bobby Thomson already aboard, the Braves had more than enough outfielders to start the season. He had a feeling he didn't have anywhere to go and told Barbara to "keep the suitcases ready."

Hank needn't have worried. He never realized that his big break would come because of another big break. Early in spring training, in an exhibition game against the Yankees in St. Petersburg, Hank was drinking a soda as he watched Bobby Thomson slide into second base. Thomson's leg folded under him, and he suffered a broken ankle. Hank watched as Thomson was carried off on a stretcher. With Thomson's ankle broken, a spot was now open. The next day, when Hank showed up for practice, Braves manager Charlie Grimm tossed him a glove and asked him to report to left field. With the toss of that glove, Hank's major-league career was about to begin.

WINTERING IN PUERTO RICO

Félix Mantilla played with Hank in Jacksonville in 1953 and would one day become his roommate when both men played for the Milwaukee Braves. After Hank and Barbara were married, Félix invited them to Puerto Rico so Hank could play winter ball for the Caguas team. Hank saw it as a good chance for him not only to play some extra ball but also, he hoped, to find out what position suited him best. After a couple of weeks into the winter season, he was batting only .125, and the team wanted to send Hank home. Félix spoke with the owner and convinced him to let Hank stay.

Because he was struggling so much at second base, team manager Mickey Owen consulted with the Milwaukee Braves and suggested Hank try the outfield. When Owen saw Hank step out there, catch the ball, throw strikes from left field to first base, it was settled. Hank was an outfielder. Owen also gave Hank some of the most valuable baseball training of his career, particularly in hitting. Hank had largely taught himself almost everything he knew about batting, and Owen gave Hank tips on crouching at the plate and hitting to more parts of the park. Also, importantly to Hank, Owen did not insist that he change the placement of his left foot at the plate!

Hank's team was in first place for most of the winter. Many of the players would eventually join the major leagues, so the competition was tough and the level of play was consistently high. In addition to helping Hank find a new position and refine his batting technique, his winter in Puerto Rico gave him a chance to play in his third All-Star game in three different leagues. Because the pitchers were so skilled, he got to practice his hitting against major-league talent. By the end of the season, he led the winter league in batting with a .337 average. He also led the league in home runs.

Playing with an Idol

At the end of spring training, the Braves joined the Brooklyn Dodgers on a preseason tour, playing games in New Orleans, Birmingham, Memphis, Louisville, and Indianapolis. For Hank, the best stop was Mobile, where he got to play in front of his biggest fans—his family. Wearing his Braves uniform with pride, Hank shared the field with Jackie Robinson. A single and a double later, Hank recalled, "I hoped my father remembered what I told him when I was 14—that I would be in the big leagues while Jackie Robinson was still there."

Although he had the honor of playing with one of his idols, Hank soon learned that life was still difficult for a black man in the major leagues. Just as had been the case during his days in the Sally League, African-American members of the Braves and the Dodgers weren't allowed to stay in the same hotels as the white players. Hank always seemed to find his way to Jackie Robinson's room. There, he was part of a different team. He belonged to the minority of African-American men in Major League Baseball.

While Hank sat and quietly read a magazine, Jackie Robinson, Don Newcombe, Roy Campanella, Joe Black, and Jim Gilliam would play cards and talk about the National League. Hank learned they had strategies for dealing with racial situations, such as when to join in a fight or how to cope when white players spit at them.

Hank remembers those hotel rooms being like a college to him—a place where he could learn from other black players about baseball,

"HANK AARON IS FABULOUS FELLOW, SAYS FORMER PILOT BEN GERAGHTY"

A *Milwaukee Journal* headline prior to the start of the 1954 season, quoting Hank's former manager at Jacksonville

OUR SPORTS

MAY 25¢

Will There Ever Be a Big League Negro Manager? by Milt Gross

A NEW MONTHLY MAGAZINE FEATURING NEGRO ATHLETES

JACKIE ROBINSON, Editor

HE CAN CHALLENGE RUTH'S HOME RUN RECORD, IF—

I JUST GAMBLED
WORLD'S GREATEST ATHLETE OF THE FUTURE?

CAN DOBY BEAT THE 2ND YEAR JINX?

WE STILL GOT OUR MEXIC-KING'S A RETIRE CHAMP

TONY ANTHONY?

LARRY DOBY

Exclusives

ROBINSON Picks the Pennant Winners
1st All-American Negro Basketball Awards
ALSO 20 ADDITIONAL FEATURES IN THE WORLD OF NEGRO SPORTS

Why Can't Negroes Wrestle in Nation's Capital?
Our Rookie Prospects

What White Big Leaguers **REALLY** Think of Negro Players—By Roork Keith

OUR SPORTS
THE NEGRO'S OWN SPORTS MAGAZINE

JACKIE ROBINSON, Editor

JUNE 25¢

THE LOWDOWN ON
HOW I CRACKED
JIM CROW GOLF
by Joe Louis

MY FEUD WITH LEO
Jackie Tells What He
Really Thinks of The Lip

MAT GLAMOR GIRLS
Bronze Wrestling Beauties
Are Terrific

MONTE THE MIGHTY
Giants Pennant Hopes
Hang On His Smith,
Ankle and Booming Bat.

MONTE IRVIN

ARE THE YANKEES ANTI-NEGRO—Here's the Lowdown—By Milton Gross

OUR SPORTS
THE NEGRO'S OWN SPORTS MAGAZINE

JACKIE ROBINSON, Editor

Here it is—
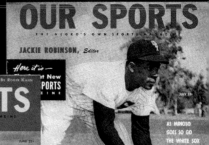
at New SPORTS ZINE

JULY 25¢

AS MINOSO
GOES SO GO
THE WHITE SOX
by Wendell Smith

MINNIE MINOSO

GRO JOCKEY — WHAT HAPPENED TO HIM?
Dominated the Tracks • But Today Is Only An Exercise Boy! WHY?

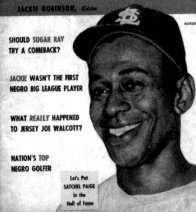

The Great New
NEGRO SPORTS
MAGAZINE

Inside Story of CARDINALS' New PRO-NEGRO Policy

OUR SPORTS

JACKIE ROBINSON, Editor

AUGUST 25¢

SHOULD SUGAR RAY
TRY A COMEBACK?

JACKIE WASN'T THE FIRST
NEGRO BIG LEAGUE PLAYER

WHAT REALLY HAPPENED
TO JERSEY JOE WALCOTT?

NATION'S TOP
NEGRO GOLFER

Let's Put
SATCHEL PAIGE
in the
Hall of Fame

BASKETBALL — BASEBALL — BOXING — TRACK — GOLF

OUR SPORTS

JACKIE ROBINSON, Editor

OCT.-NOV. 25¢

The Great New
NEGRO SPORTS
MAGAZINE

ALL-AMERICAN
FOOTBALL PREVIEW

WHY ARE NEGRO STARS STILL
BURIED IN THE MINORS?

THE REAL STORY
OF RANDY TURPIN

TOP NEGRO BASKETBALL
PLAYERS FOR THIS
SEASON - PROFESSIONAL AND COLLEGIATE

In the early 1950s, Our Sports, a magazine that billed itself as "The Great New Negro Sports Magazine," appeared briefly, with editorial contributions from Jackie Robinson and various respected writers. Its first cover (upper left) shows Larry Doby, who broke the American League color line with the Cleveland Indians in 1947, several months after Robinson made his debut with the National League Brooklyn Dodgers.

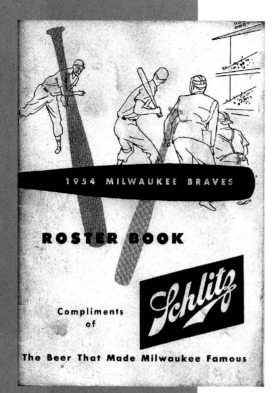

1954 MILWAUKEE BRAVES

ROSTER BOOK

Compliments of Schlitz

The Beer That Made Milwaukee Famous

This complimentary souvenir booklet was available to fans during the 1954 season, the Braves' second in Milwaukee and Hank's first in the majors. It contained sketches of every member of the team, including the one of Hank, shown opposite.

pride, and life. Spending time with the Dodgers, listening to their stories and guidance, Hank soon realized what it meant to be a minority in a professional sport:

"I could never be just another major-league player. I was a black player, and that meant I would be separate most of the time from most of the players on the team. It meant I'd better be good, or I'd be gone. It meant that some players and some fans would hate me no matter what I did."

He also learned that although it was difficult, he was never going to forget or ignore his roots.

Despite all of the changes, Hank eventually became acclimated to his new life in the major leagues. His first big-league hit was against Vic Raschi of the Cardinals, a game-winning double in Milwaukee on April 15. Eight days after that, Hank hammered his first homer in St. Louis, once again against Raschi. He even found that "playing in the big leagues wasn't nearly as hard as getting there."

The Braves drew a lot of attention in 1954, Hank's rookie year. Fans arrived

"I'M A QUIET BOY..."

f the first depictions of Hank as a Milwaukee Brave includes t
"Henry," the name he grew up using and actually preferred.
eatment Hank received in Milwaukee was certainly more racia
t than during his year in the Sally League. The talk balloon,
er, is a reminder of the fact that baseball as a whole was still
that far removed from its segregationist past, and the nation
e still had a way to go in becoming more racially sensitive. H

in carloads, hung out at pregame tailgate parties, and then went into the ballpark to cheer on their beloved Braves. By August, the team had set a National League attendance record, and they finished the year with what was at the time a whopping 2.1 million in attendance. Hank knew he wasn't the star attraction—at least not yet. Players like the Braves' own Eddie Mathews, along with established stars such as Jackie Robinson and Willie Mays, were gracing the headlines and the covers of *Sports Illustrated*. Meanwhile, Hank was known as the "guy filling in for Bobby Thomson."

Filling in or not, Hank had a decent rookie season that ended a few weeks early when, sliding in for a triple on September 5, he broke his ankle the same way Thomson had. Stuck in a cast for most of the winter, Hank played with his young daughter and looked forward to a new season. Once his cast was removed, he had his brother, Tommie, pitch to him in Carver Park. It was time to get ready for the upcoming season.

BROTHERS IN ARMS: HANK AND TOMMIE AARON

During the winter following the 1954 season, Tommie Aaron helped his brother, Hank, prepare for the upcoming Braves season by pitching to him at Carver Park. At the time, Tommie was only 15, and Hank had no idea his younger brother would someday join him in the major leagues. Tommie signed with the Braves in 1958, at the age of 18. When he came up to the Braves in 1962, he and Hank became the first siblings to play together in a League Championship Series. Later, after spending some more time in the minors, Tommie joined his brother again on the Atlanta Braves, in 1968. His playing career ended in 1971, but he spent several years managing in the minor leagues and coaching with Atlanta.

In 1982, during a physical exam given to Braves staff members, doctors discovered that Tommie had leukemia. Despite receiving treatment, Tommie passed away in 1984. He left behind his wife, Carolyn, and three children. Even though he had been unable to reach his full potential in coaching due to his untimely death, Tommie Aaron is etched in history alongside his brother. On July 11, 1962, the brothers hit homers in the same inning of the same game—something that hadn't been done since 1932.

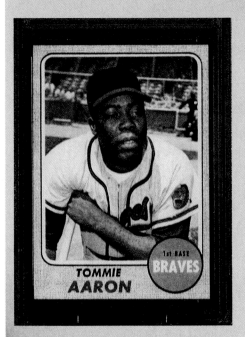

TOMMIE AARON
1st BASE BRAVES

Tommie Aaron's trading card for 1968, the year he rejoined the Braves (who had by then moved to Atlanta) after several years playing for the Richmond Braves in the International League.

Chapter 4
The All-Around Brave

When he returned in 1955, Hank knew there would be some changes in his second season. Bobby Thomson had recovered and taken over his old post in left field, so Hank was asked to move to right. Hank also decided to make another change—he asked for the number 44. Previously, he had worn number 5, but he felt it didn't suit him. When he approached the team's traveling secretary, Donald Davidson, for a two-digit number, Davidson laughed and said that Hank was far too skinny to carry around such a big number. He did, however, agree to the request, and Hank sported the number 44.

Along with a new number, the 1955 season also earned Hank a new nickname—Hammerin' Hank.

Hammerin' Hank Comes into His Own

In 1955, Hank showed the team that he could handle the weight of his new number. Slim build or not, the first half of his season earned him an appearance in the All-Star game. It was Hank's first All-Star game of what would become 24 All-Star appearances. By the end of the season, he was batting .314, had hit 27 home runs, and had 106 RBIs. He was also named the team's MVP. Hank's improvement paralleled that of the Braves, who finished the year in second place. They just couldn't squeeze past the Dodgers.

Along with a new number, the 1955 season also earned Hank a new nickname— Hammerin' Hank. A sportswriter in New York used the name in a column mentioning one of Hank's homers, and it caught on like wildfire. Davidson helped spread the nickname, encouraging other reporters to use it.

Barnstorming with the Negro League All-Stars

Between the end of spring training and the official start of the 1956 season, Hank decided to join a team made up of major-league African-American players barnstorming its way north and playing against a team of Negro League All-Stars. Hank remembers the sheer excitement of playing for such a great team. "We didn't lose. I mean we didn't ever lose," Hank later gushed. "That might have been the best team ever assembled." He also had the incredible experience of getting to know and form close ties with Willie Mays of the Giants, Don Newcombe of the Dodgers, and other

Hank strikes an on-deck pose for this official Braves photo, taken sometime in the mid- to late 1950s

fellow players, building both competitions and friendships while barnstorming together.

"Ol' Hank Is Ready"

When the 1956 season came around, Hank stepped out of the batting cage during spring training one day and announced, "Ol' Hank is ready." He was eager to start hammerin' again, and the newspapers picked up on that eagerness, doing their part to rev up fan support.

Hank was ready, all right. The Braves hit a bit of a rough spot in the early weeks of the season but, by June, they had won their 11th straight game. This winning streak had propelled them into first place, and Hank was also on a streak of his own, contributing to the excitement by hitting safely in 25 consecutive games. Milwaukee fans were ecstatic about their team. They couldn't get enough.

It was as if the team and the city were seized with pennant fever from the start of the season. "The whole state became excited about the Braves," Hank recalled. "There were Braves hairdos, Braves cocktails, and Braves banners stretched across the streets." Of course, the real object of the heightened excitement— and expectations—was the World Series. Everybody, including the Braves themselves, thought they'd make it to the World Series.

With hopes running so high, realities can hit hard. Despite Milwaukee's best efforts, Brooklyn was simply too strong a team. The Braves fell one game behind them on the last weekend of the season, finishing with a 92–62 record. Although the rest of the team, and the city, were heartbroken, Hank saw something

Hank Aaron rounds third against the Brooklyn
Dodgers, sometime during the summer of 1956.
Despite Milwaukee's 12-games-to-10 season wins
over Brooklyn, the season, full of high hopes and
expectations, ended with a thud when the team
finished one game behind the Dodgers in the final
standings. With that, the Braves narrowly missed a
trip to the World Series. It would take another year
for the bitter disappointment to become transformed
into the sheer, unbridled ecstasy of the fall of 1957.

positive in their loss: "It was Jackie Robinson's last season in the big leagues, and it was only fitting that he got to go out in a World Series."

Despite his team finishing in second place for the second year in a row, Hank reached some personal milestones. His .328 batting average made him the second-youngest batting champion in National League history. He also surpassed the 20-homer mark for the second consecutive season. He led the NL in hits and

In 1956 during Robinson's last season, Hank knew Major League Baseball was losing a key figure. Now more than ever, he wanted to represent who he was with dignity and pride.

doubles, with 200 and 34, respectively. He also received some more public attention when *The Sporting News* named him NL Player of the Year. Coming as they did from "the Bible of Baseball," *TSN* Player of the Year awards were considered by many fans to be in a class all their own as way of honoring performance.

Hank was also beginning to trust his own instincts as a player. He was proud to be around at a time when he could step up as a representative of his team and help advance the cause of equality in the game he loved so much.

FREE ON THE TRAIN

As they traveled from city to city for their games, the Braves used various forms of transportation. Hank remembers the train as a special place. Always wanting to learn from other players, black or white, Hank enjoyed the desegregation of the train. "The train was about the only place where I got a chance to sit and talk with the white players," he recalled of the earlier days of his career in professional baseball, especially before air travel became common.

His friend and teammate Eddie Mathews also remembers his time on the train and the tension of the times:

"The train gave us all a chance to be together.... [W]e would gather in there with a couple cases of beer and stay up into the wee hours.... It was rough on the black players. We all knew the situation was ridiculous—especially spring training. As I look back on it now, I realized I should have done more about it than I did—we all should have."

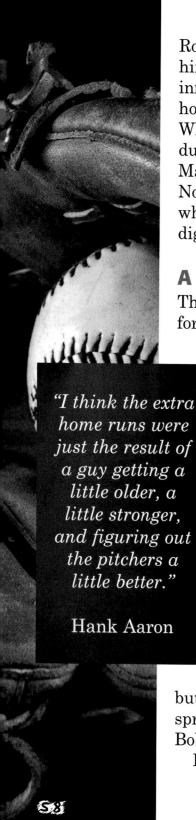

Many times while playing the Braves, Jackie Robinson would pull Hank aside and talk with him about the game. Hank soaked up all the information he could from his idol and was honored that Jackie thought he had promise. When the Dodgers won the pennant in 1956 during Robinson's last season, Hank knew Major League Baseball was losing a key figure. Now, more than ever, he wanted to represent who he was as a player and an individual with dignity and pride.

A Banner Year

The 1957 season started out fast and strong for the Braves. With a home run in the season opener and five singles a few days later, Hank was in on all the action. By June, he had hit seven homers in eight days. Although he never thought of himself as a home run hitter (he left that to super-stars like Willie Mays), people began equating Hank with homers. Many of his teammates even thought he was competing for home runs, but Hank believed it was just a matter of getting older and wiser.

"I think the extra home runs were just the result of a guy getting a little older, a little stronger, and figuring out the pitchers a little better."

Hank Aaron

Team changes mid-season brought some familiar faces to the Braves. Hank's Eau Claire teammate Wes Covington and his old friend Félix Mantilla joined the team. Hank enjoyed being reunited with his old teammates, but soon had to sit out a few days to nurse a sprained ankle. The Braves also acquired rookie Bob "Hurricane" Hazle for the stretch run.

In August, the Braves put together a ten-game winning streak and found themselves with an eight-and-a-half game lead with 40 games left to play. With their new players, including "Hurricane" Hazle, they were blowing the league away. After losing the pennant race in the 11th hour in 1956, however, nobody was taking their position for granted this time.

Despite keeping their heads in the game, they started to lose ground. The Cardinals were gaining on the Braves' lead, and they gave Milwaukee a run for the pennant. On September 23, the Braves and the Cardinals were tied, 2–2, in extra innings. At the bottom of the 11th, Johnny Logan of the Braves was on first when Hank stepped up to bat. Hank knew that if he could get Logan home, the Braves would win the game. He faced Billy Muffett on the mound. Muffett was a pitcher who hadn't given up a single homer all season long.

When Muffett threw a breaking ball his way, Hank hammered it past center field and into a grove of pine trees. Dashing around the bases, Hank knew they had the pennant. His teammates of course knew this, too, and when Hank reached home, they jubilantly hoisted him onto their shoulders and carried him off the field. Hank remembers that home run as his greatest moment in baseball. "I've never had another feeling like that."

The next day, Hank hammered out his 44th homer, a grand slam against the Cardinals. With that HR, he solidified his first home run title. He also earned the league's RBI title that season, with 132. Had he finished first in batting average as well, he would have won baseball's Triple Crown. Instead, he finished

third (with .322), behind superstars Stan Musial and Willie Mays. Although Hank badly wanted to win the Triple Crown, he focused on what lay ahead of him. After all, he and the Braves were on their way to the World Series.

The World Series

Entering into the World Series, the Braves were up against the New York Yankees. Despite the Braves' pennant-winning performance, the Yanks were clear favorites in the Series. Winning 17 previous world championships, they looked like an unstoppable, invincible force. By contrast, the Braves had only won a single pennant. Some of the Yankees voiced their confidence loudly, calling the Braves and Milwaukee "bush," a reference to the Braves and their hometown as minor league, or inferior to the big-city New Yorkers.

Hank and the rest of the Braves couldn't let the Yankees get to them. They were determined to win, despite New York's lineup of intimidating hitters, including Yogi Berra, Hank Bauer, and Mickey Mantle, and corps of outstanding pitchers, such as Whitey Ford and Don Larsen, who had pitched a perfect game against the Dodgers in the Series one year ago.

In Yankee Stadium, the Yanks won game one, 3–1. In game two, the Braves got the scoring going in the second inning when Hank tripled over Mickey Mantle's head in center field and then scored on Joe Adcock's single. The Braves went on to take game two, 4–2.

One little-known piece of trivia related to that victory is that every single *game* in every World Series between 1948 and 1957 had been won by a team from New York. The Yankees in the American League and the former National League New York Giants and Brooklyn Dodgers were dominant in the decade preceding 1957, until the Braves broke the spell with their win in that second game of the 1957 Series.

Game three took place in Milwaukee. Despite a homer by Hank, the Braves couldn't hold their game together and lost by a whopping 12–3. The Yanks now held a two-games-to-one lead. In game four, the Braves blew an early lead and the Yankees tied it up in the ninth inning. Just when it looked as if

Riding on their momentum, the Braves took game five, 1–0. Soon, they were on their way to New York for game six.

the Braves were going to fall behind three games to one, a pitch in the bottom of the 10th inning by Yankee pitcher Tommy Byrne wound up at Braves player Nippy Jones' feet.

It was one pitch, but it changed the course of the Series. Jones began to argue with the umpire, claiming that the ball had hit him. Only when Jones convinced the umpire that a spot of shoe polish on the ball was caused by the ball hitting him on the foot, was he allowed to head to first base. Teammate Johnny Logan

then hit a double to tie the game. Finally, Eddie Mathews slammed a homer that won the game. The Series was now tied at two wins apiece.

Riding on their momentum, the Braves took game five, 1–0. Soon, they were on their way to New York for game six. If they won, the series would be over and the Braves would be world champions. Victory was so close, they could almost taste it. Even as they were stuck in a traffic jam on the busy New York streets while headed to the game, they were thinking only of becoming world champions.

Hank knew he had to stay at the top of his game to help his team. So he did what he did best. At the top of the seventh inning, he smashed a home run. It helped tie the game at 2–2. Then, at the bottom of the seventh, Yankee outfielder Hank Bauer scored a run, giving the Yankees a one-run lead. They took game six, winning 3–2 over the Braves.

Happy Days Are Here!

It all came down to game seven, again at Yankee Stadium. From the start, Milwaukee was on fire. After just three innings, the Braves were leading 4–0. Starting pitcher Lew Burdette shut out the Yankees, and the Braves took the game with a final score of 5–0. Now the team the Yanks had called "bush league" had officially become the best team in baseball. The Milwaukee Braves had won their first World Series title.

The city of Milwaukee could hardly contain its excitement. Fans swarmed the streets of downtown Milwaukee, where one hand-lettered

October 6, 1957. Hank Aaron returns to
the dugout after hitting a home run for the
Milwaukee Braves in inning four of game
four of the 1957 World Series in Milwaukee.
The Braves went on to win that game in
extra innings, 7–5, on the famous "shoe
polish" play, and eventually took the
Series, seven games to six.

sign that made news stories all over the country proclaimed, "Bushville Wins." The Braves had become the toast of the town.

Although Hank batted .393 for the Series, pitcher Burdette was named MVP. But Hank didn't go unrecognized. A few weeks later, he was named National League MVP. He was delighted to be selected: "For me, it was one thing to perform well—I always knew I could do that—but it was another thing to be appreciated for it." At 23 years old, with a World Series ring on his finger, Hank was having the best year of his baseball life. "It doesn't get any better than Milwaukee in 1957," he later said.

The 1957–1958 Off-Season

Hank was also making plans to celebrate at home. Soon, he would be a dad again. He and Barbara had a growing family. Three-year-old Gaile was living in Mobile with her grandmother, and son Hank Jr. (Hankie) had arrived after the 1957 pennant drive. Barbara was pregnant again, this time with twins. The boys, Gary and Larry, were born prematurely on December 15, 1957. Sadly, Gary died in the hospital.

The Aarons brought Larry to Hank's mother in Mobile, where he started to gain strength and improve. Hank didn't like being away from his children, so he and his wife spent a lot of time traveling from Milwaukee to Mobile.

It was also at this time that Hank became even more interested in the civil rights movement. He became friends with Father Mike Sablica, a white Catholic priest in Milwaukee. Together, they talked about discrimination,

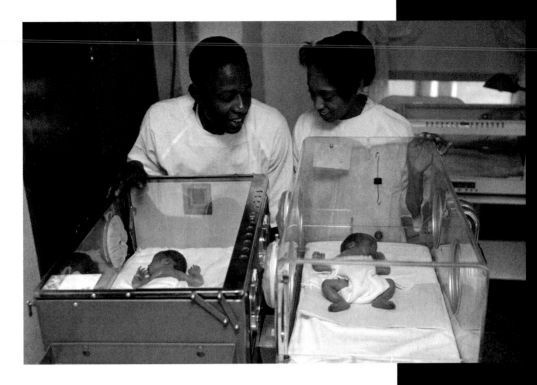

human rights, and life in general. Eventually, he and Sablica became very close, learning from each other's experiences.

The Key to the City

After his World Series win, Hank was invited back to Mobile for Hank Aaron Day. He was honored by the mayor and given the key to the city. "That was a proud day for all the black people of Mobile—a kid from Toulminville being honored by the mayor himself," Hank recalled.

He was also asked to speak at an all-white men's club in Mobile. He wanted to bring his father along, but the club wouldn't allow it. Said Hank:

"It was one thing for a black World Series hero to speak to their club, but it was another

Hank and Barbara look in on their twin boys Larry (left) and Gary, shown here in their incubators. The boys were born in December 1957 in Milwaukee. They were born prematurely, each weighing less than 3.5 pounds (1.6 kg). Sadly, Gary passed away in the hospital.

thing to have his black daddy sitting with all the good white men in the audience."

Hank was frustrated and canceled the engagement. The more he experienced racism, the more he felt driven to challenge the world around him.

As the 1958 season approached, the Braves were looking ahead to defending their title. They starting by winning the NL pennant by eight games over the Pittsburgh Pirates.

Hank also had another solid season. He finished with a .326 average, 95 RBIs, and 30 homers. He made another trip to the All-Star game and won a Gold Glove at the end of the season. This award goes to the league's best fielder at each position. With Gold Glove winners Hank Aaron and catcher Del Crandall aboard, the Braves made their way to their second World Series.

There, they again squared off against the New York Yankees. The Yankees were a strong team, but the Braves dominated the early part of the Series and put together a 3–1 lead in games. Victory was within reach, but the team just couldn't hold onto their commanding lead. "For whatever reason, we just didn't seem like quite the same team despite the fact that we were every bit as good in '58 as we had been in '57," Hank later noted. The Yankees came back to win the last three games. Hank had a solid batting average (.333), but he'd hit no home runs and only two RBIs during the entire Series. Hank tried not to let the numbers get to him, remembering that he was just starting out and probably had better years ahead—and he was right.

In the 1959 season, Hank's determination and solid focus were starting to pay off. He was batting remarkably well, hitting .508 through April. In May, he was still above .450. Even he knew he had never been better. "I was seeing the ball so well that I stopped going to the movies for a while, because I didn't want anything to affect my eyes," he remembered.

By September, the Braves were tied for first in the league against some familiar faces. The Dodgers had moved to Los Angeles in 1957, but they were once again the main obstacle to a Braves pennant. On the last weekend of the season, LA lost to the Cubs, while the Braves beat Philadelphia. This pulled them into a tie with LA and a three-game playoff for the pennant. The Dodgers were a weaker team than in their earlier days, so the Braves were confident.

In game one, at Milwaukee County Stadium, the Braves scored two runs in the first inning, but the Dodgers came back and tied it and then went ahead for good on a home run by John Roseboro in the sixth.

Game two started like game one, with the Braves taking an early lead. After taking the game to extra innings, the Dodgers bested the Braves and went to the World Series. Their season was over. Worse yet: no pennant would be flying over County Stadium next year.

SPORT Magazine '58 ALL STAR Selection

HANK AARON
RIGHT FIELD • NATIONAL LEAGUE

Looking back, Hank knew that the Braves could have performed better: "I wish I knew what kept us from winning more, because there is no question that we had the talent—three Hall of Famers, and that was just a start.... Besides that, half our guys would fight their mothers to win a baseball game." Despite the disappointment of losing the pennant, however, Hank had a lot more baseball in him.

Just Getting Started

By the late 1950s and early 1960s, Major League Baseball had been integrated for a little over a decade. Of the ten MVPs named in the 1950s, eight were African-American. The black players made up less than eight percent of the players on major-league teams, and they were just getting started. The same could be said for Hank, as he swung his way into 1960, winning his second batting title in 1959 and leading the league with 233 hits. He was also the second-youngest player to reach 1,000 hits. But Hank was most proud of the 400 total bases he racked up that year.

Hank was growing and maturing both as a player and as a citizen interested in civil rights. He remembered the mid-sixties as a peak time for African-American ball players. "We were the Jackie Robinson generation," he recalled.

It was also at this time that Martin Luther King Jr. led a quarter of a million people in the March on Washington and delivered his now-famous "I Have a Dream" speech. The racial climate of the time was a constantly changing thing. It became more important for Hank to see his team together, both black and white players, under the same roof. Both literally and symbolically, it meant staying at the same hotel. This focus—equal treatment for all team members—would soon become even more of a reality for Hank than he could have imagined.

In the early 1960s, the Braves began to lose much of their luster. Hank did more than his share with his bat, hitting for average, home runs, and RBIs, and pitcher Warren Spahn continued to win close to or more than 20 games a year. The team on the whole was not keeping pace with Aaron and Spahn, however. Although they continued to post winning records, they were nowhere near the "glory years" of the 1950s. The team was sold in 1962 to a group that was reportedly in search of a market with a larger TV audience. Atlanta was busy trying to lure big-league baseball to the South, and the club soon became the object of a legal battle between Milwaukee and the Braves. The team had planned to move in 1965, but a court order would keep it in Milwaukee until 1966. Everybody knew this would only delay the inevitable. Hank and the Braves would soon be on their way down South—to Atlanta, Georgia.

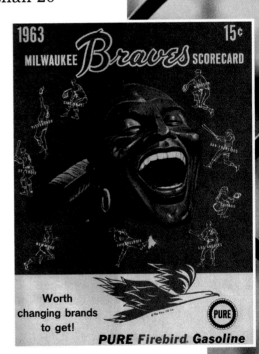

The "Screaming Indian" adorned sleeves and score-cards of the Milwaukee and Atlanta Braves from the 1950s until the mid-1980s. It was discontinued in part due to concerns over its use of stereotyped images of Native people.

Chapter 5
A Change of Scenery—and Bearing Down on the Babe

The Braves were a contending team in 1965, their final season in Milwaukee, but the city of Milwaukee didn't seem to have the heart for it. Fans were so dispirited by the desertion of a team with which they had had a love affair for over a decade, that they stayed away from County Stadium in droves. Some boycotted the team, while others simply couldn't stand being in a place that had once given them so much joy and now felt like a death watch. So deep was the fans' feeling of betrayal by their beloved Braves, that attendance in that final season dropped to 555,584—a far, far cry from the 2,215,404 fans who helped power the Braves' championship season in 1957. The Braves were also losing Félix Mantilla, Wes Covington, and other favorites who had been traded to other teams.

1966: Not in Milwaukee Anymore
Hank continued to hit well during that last season in Milwaukee, bagging 32 homers and

batting .318. He and Eddie Mathews set a mark for the most combined career home runs hit by teammates—773. (By the end of the following season—their first in Atlanta and Eddie's last as a Brave—the two sluggers had hit a grand total of 863 home runs as teammates.) But even this remarkable performance by one of the game's greatest one-two punches neither received much publicity from the local media nor excited the interest of the jaded fan base.

Hank and Barbara weren't eager to go to Atlanta. Packing up and moving to a segregated southern town was daunting, but the thought of being closer to Mobile and his family was tempting to both of them. They eventually bought a nice ranch house on two acres (0.8 hectare) of land in an African-American community. The move went well, but they were reminded they weren't in Milwaukee anymore. It was during his time in Atlanta that Hank began receiving letters in the mail.

When Hank and the Braves arrived in Atlanta for the 1966 season, he knew his career was going to change. Back home in Milwaukee, he was a genuine fan favorite. In Atlanta, he could feel the racial tension, just as

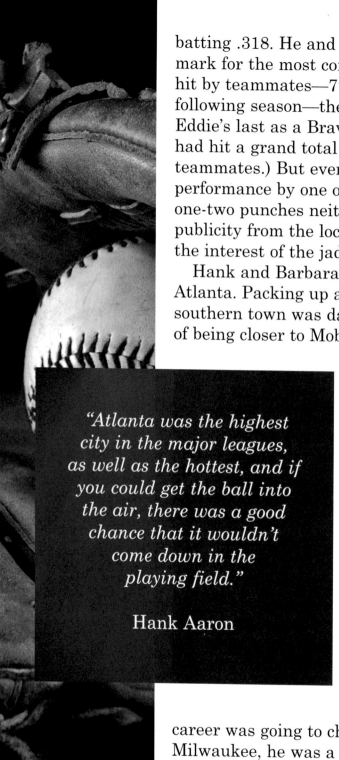

"Atlanta was the highest city in the major leagues, as well as the hottest, and if you could get the ball into the air, there was a good chance that it wouldn't come down in the playing field."

Hank Aaron

he had years earlier in the Sally League.
But Hank was determined to turn the move
to Atlanta into an opportunity to be part of a
community, and he believed he could connect
with the crowd by hitting home runs. As he
put it, "I needed a decisive way to win over the
white people before they thought of a reason
to hate me."

When Hank started playing in Atlanta, he
had a .320 lifetime batting average, the highest
in the National League among active players.

*The Braves' first season in Atlanta was a
lot like their last one in Milwaukee—
solid, but not spectacular.*

When Hank failed to score a single run in
the Braves' opening home game, he grew
desperate to hit that first home run. Luckily,
he quickly found his groove.

Soon, he was swinging away again. The
air was different in Atlanta, and he learned
how to work with it. The city's relatively
high altitude and warmer climate helped
give his hits "lift," carrying them farther into
the stands.

The Braves' first season in Atlanta was a
lot like their last one in Milwaukee—solid,
but not spectacular. Hank and two other
players—Felipe Alou and Joe Torre—hit

HANK AARON

more than 30 homers each, and others contributed their fair share. Atlanta soon became known as the home run capital of baseball. Still, the Braves couldn't seriously contend for the pennant because of their poor pitching.

Tension On and Off the Field

At the time, Atlanta was the only southern city with a major-league team, so the racial tension was worse at home than on the road. Often, Hank's wife and children suffered verbal abuse while watching him from the stands. Hank began to speak up more and more, defending himself from prejudice on the field. He remembered,

"I was changing fast, and it started when we moved to Atlanta. Atlanta changed me as a hitter and a person at the same time."

Hank and Barbara began to drift apart, and their marriage suffered. This was also the first time Hank seriously began thinking about going after Babe Ruth's home run record. "I was tired of being invisible," he noted.

The 1967 season was a tough one for Hank, on and off the field. He played on despite a house fire, some run-ins with fans, the press, and even a teammate, Rico Carty, on a Braves' charter flight that involved a wise crack being taken seriously. Hank led the league in home runs, extra-base hits, and runs scored, and he brought his average back above .300.

In 1968, Hank reached a new milestone. After years of consistently high home run totals, he hit his 500th in August. Many consider this milestone one that may have started some people calculating the possibility of this relatively quiet, unspectacular ballplayer actually having a shot at Babe Ruth's all-time HR record. While this meant a great deal to Hank, other events continued to influence his perception of himself as an athlete and a human being. One of these was the assassination of Martin Luther King Jr. earlier that year in Memphis. As Hank reached new heights in baseball, he thought a lot about the effect he

"I'm not so sure that everyone forgot my color, but I'd like to think that I had a small hand in bringing Atlanta into the modern era."

OUTFIELD

might have on others. Dr. King had been a great influence on Hank, and now Hank felt a desire to contribute to the world in his own positive way. "I'm not so sure that everyone forgot my color, but I'd like to think that I had a small hand in bringing Atlanta into the modern era," he recalled.

By the 1969 season, Hank was beginning

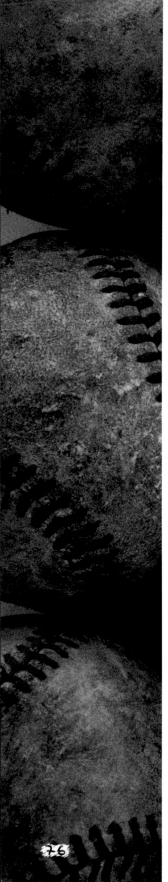

to think about his legacy as a ballplayer. At 35, he was getting close to a player's normal retirement age. He even knew that his name would be in the record books for hits, home runs, totals bases, and RBIs. His lifetime average going into the 1969 season was .314—again, the highest of all active players. The Braves were even pennant contenders for the first time in years. But he knew that to ordinary people who didn't pore over record books, his name wouldn't be said along with Babe Ruth's unless he did something bigger and better. Retirement age or not, Hank wasn't quite ready to give up.

Neither were the Braves. The team moved into first place on September 17, beating the Dodgers in 12 innings. Nine wins in a row later, they were in the playoffs and, yet, Hank picked up on something not quite "right" about his teammates' frame of mind going into the NL post-season. Their opponents, the New York Mets, had won 100 games that year and had a strong pitching staff. Still, the Braves were considered the favorites, and yet Hank noticed that many of his teammates had a defeatist attitude from the get-go.

In game one, the Braves led in the seventh, but the Mets came back with five runs and the win. In game two, Hank homered in the fifth, but it wasn't enough, and the Mets took the win. Game three took place in New York. Hammering another home run, Hank gave Atlanta a 2–0 lead in the first inning. Despite that early lead, the Mets won the game and swept the playoff round with three straight wins. Hank compared the defeat to the Braves' pennant losses to the Dodgers in 1956 and 1959. During those times, he knew the Braves shouldn't have lost. But this time was different: "...[T]he Mets jumped all over us in the '69 playoffs, and when they were through, we knew we'd been up against more than we could handle."

After Hank's strong performance in a losing cause, people began to regard him a little differently. He felt that they treated him with a bit of sympathy. With fellow ballplayers on their way to retirement, he wondered if people now saw him as an old man playing a younger man's game.

Mr. 3,000

For years, Hank yearned to reach his goal of 3,000 career hits. It was the number in the back of his head, urging him forward through difficult times and games. It wasn't enough for Hank to be a great hitter. Getting 3,000 hits meant you had proven yourself as solid against injury, bad luck, and aging. In a word, it meant *consistency*. In 1970, Hank finally made it to the exclusive 3,000 hit club.

It happened during a doubleheader at Cincinnati. It was a fitting place for this milestone, as Crosley Field was where he had played his first major-league game. After the hit, his friend Stan Musial of the Cardinals joined him on the field to celebrate. Stan was the only living member of the 3,000 club, and Hank was eager to join a man whom he admired so much.

His 3,000th hit brought Hank more attention and fanfare. The Braves held a

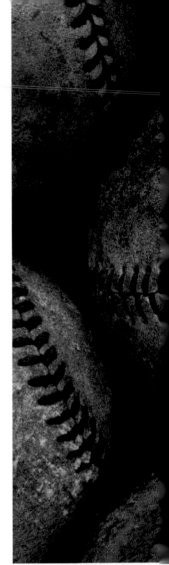

"day" for him to celebrate the occasion, and Hank was showered with gifts, from a year's supply of Coca-Cola to a golf cart with the number 44 on it. He was featured on the cover of *Sports Illustrated* magazine. His favorite prize was the ball he hit, which he donated to the Baseball Hall of Fame.

Shortly after the fanfare died down, Hank was eager to carry on playing ball. He had another, less formal achievement to celebrate during the 1970 season. In a game against the San Francisco Giants, Hank hit the first home run to land in the left-field upper deck of Atlanta Stadium. To note the event, the Braves painted a gold hammer on the seat that marked the spot. It was a great moment in the season for Hank, who finished with 38 homers,

In 1971, Hank hit his 600th homer. He was gaining ground on the home run record held by Ruth.

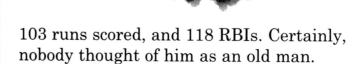

103 runs scored, and 118 RBIs. Certainly, nobody thought of him as an old man.

Hank continued to chase home runs. Shortly after Hank collected his 3,000th hit, Willie Mays hit his. Hank had always felt a friendly rivalry with Mays and although he was proud to reach the 3,000 milestone ahead of Willie, he was still about 40 home runs behind him.

Hank Aaron collects his 3,000th career hit during a game between the Braves and the Cincinnati Reds at Crosley Field in Cincinnati on May 17, 1970.

Hank never wanted to be seen as second best and began to put more into hitting homers.

With all of his energy directed at hitting the home run, Hank's life began to change. "As I drew closer to Willie and Ruth, I fell farther away from Barbara," he remembered. It was around this time that his wife filed for divorce.

The divorce was hard on everybody, including, of course, his children. Having a famous father was difficult, and Hank worked hard to raise them properly. Barbara had custody of their kids, so Hank traveled a lot between his apartment and their house for visits. He turned to his close friends to get him through the tough time. He also turned his focus on hitting home runs.

In 1971, Hank hit his 600th homer. He was gaining ground on the home run record held by Ruth. Fans and the media were reluctant to

Hank enjoyed the new, younger players, but having his old friend back helped ground him.

accept Hank as the one who might challenge the Babe. They expected a charismatic, "in-your-face" player like Mickey Mantle or Willie Mays. Nobody expected the quieter, shyer Aaron. It wasn't until that spring of 1971 that people began to see that Hank just might do it.

Chasing the Babe

Although it should have been one of the happiest times in his life, chasing the home run record was one of the toughest. Hank soon found out that hitting home runs was a great way to release pent-up emotions. Although he had close friends who made him laugh, he was rarely happy and spent a lot of time moping. Even when Hank signed a two-year contract for $200,000 to stay with the Braves, he felt alone.

Halfway through the 1972 season, Hank reached another record previously attained by the Babe. This one was Ruth's record for home runs hit by a player with one team. Hank's 660th home run took place in Cincinnati, against Wayne Simpson of the Reds. People were starting to believe he could catch Ruth and started to cheer him on. When he broke Stan Musial's all-time total base record the same year, Hank became even more famous.

Everybody wanted to interview Hank, and he dealt with magazines and television reporters nearly every day. The Braves had to hire a secretary to handle his mail and schedule interviews. Hank wasn't used to such attention, and he didn't really enjoy it. He also didn't want younger players to think he was showboating. To avoid upsetting his teammates, he made a point of sharing his time with the other players.

Hank felt that his life had started changing for the better, and he was slowly starting to feel normal again. His former teammate Eddie Mathews returned to the Braves as manager in 1972, and Hank felt at home once again. He enjoyed the new, younger players, but having his old friend back helped ground him. It was

also at this time that Hank's life took another surprising turn—he met a woman.

A Life-Changing Interview

Billye Williams was a recent widower and co-host of a talk show called *Today in Georgia*. Wanting to profile the Braves, she had contacted Hank for an interview. Hank initially missed his scheduled interview, but he was rebooked. After his interview, he asked Billye out to dinner, and the two became close. Soon, they were in love.

Hank felt he became a better person with Billye. He learned to better express himself and the things he believed in, and she supported him fully. He would need it—the closer he got to Ruth's record, the more hate mail he received.

Late in October of 1972, Hank's resolve to beat the record solidified. Jackie Robinson died a few weeks after speaking in Cincinnati. Hank was appalled to see how few active baseball players attended his funeral, and he vowed to keep Jackie's dream alive. Hank knew that everybody, black and white, had a place in baseball, and the only way he could show it was to keep swinging.

Hank was eager to begin his 1973 season. He had Billye at his side and Mathews behind him all the way. He tried not to let the hundreds of hate letters impede his concentration on the game. Seven of his first nine hits were homers, but his batting average dropped to .200. Critics were outraged, believing that Hank only cared about the home run record. Hank quickly decided that his new goal would be to hit .300 that year. If the record didn't come, he still had next year. The last thing he wanted was to be known as a poor hitter who could only hit HRs.

As he kept swinging, the racist comments surrounded him everywhere. He would be heckled on the field and slammed by baseball fans. They told him he had no right to break Babe Ruth's record. Often, the FBI had to confiscate his mail because it had become a physical threat to himself and his family. At one point, Hank and Billye met with the FBI and learned that his daughter, Gaile, had been the victim of an attempted kidnapping. Hank issued a public statement about how disappointed he was with the whole situation. He decided to focus on the fans who encouraged him and, in some way, this plan helped him. His average actually began climbing.

Even so, Hank soon became overwhelmed by all the hatred surrounding him. In May, he finally mentioned the hate mail to a reporter in Philadelphia, and he received an instant boost. Thousands of people began writing positive letters to him, and the National League rallied to his side. By the year's end, he had received 93,000 letters. The majority of them were encouraging.

In late July, Hank hit his 700th home run. Ruth's record sat at 714, so Hank knew he was getting there. He smiled as he rounded third base. "There was something about getting there that made me feel I was almost at my

"Dear Hank, I understand you get a lot of crank letters concerning breaking Ruth's record. Enclosed is something [matches taped to the page] that will take care of those letters."

***

"Dear Mr. Aaron, I am 12 years old, and I wanted to tell you that I have read many articles about the prejudice against you. I really think it's bad. I don't care what color you are. You could be green and it wouldn't matter."

From letters of support written to Hank Aaron

destination, like I had been traveling the back roads for 20 years and suddenly I was on Ruth's street ..." he recalled. Soon after, *Newsweek* magazine named Hank the most conspicuous figure in sports.

Certainly, Hank was conspicuous, and he still felt the weight of negative attention. On the night of his 711th homer, there were only 1,362 fans in the stands. It was the smallest crowd in Braves history, yet the rest of the country was glued to the news as they watched the Ruth Chase. Outside Atlanta, Hank had become the center of a national event.

Wanting to tie the Babe's record before winter, Hank went into his final game on a Sunday with mixed emotions. He was proud of his season, hitting 40 homers and driving in almost 100 runs. He had even achieved his batting average goal and was sitting close to .300. But he wanted the pressure to be off over the winter. He also had plans to marry Billye. Unfortunately, no one would go home with the thrill of experiencing home run number 714— not Hank, not the fans, and not the media.

The game did hold one surprise for Hank, however, and it came from the stands. As he made his way to left field for the ninth inning, the fans began to rise. The biggest crowd of the season stood and cheered for Hank for a full five minutes. It was one of the happiest, most moving moments of Hank's life. Although he had to wait another six months for his shot at the record, his fans helped keep his spirits high.

Over the winter, Hank and Billye were married and traveled all over the United States. He was honored at banquets and visited with friends. The buzz of the Ruth Chase had

THE COMMISSIONER STEPS IN

In the photo below, Hank Aaron stands holding a trophy presented to him by baseball commissioner Bowie Kuhn before the second game of the Braves' 1974 opening series in Cincinnati. On the previous night, Hank had tied Babe Ruth's record for career home runs at 714. The Braves' management, wanting to increase the chances that Hank would break Ruth's record before the Atlanta fans, had decided to have Hank sit out the entire series with Cincinnati, but Kuhn insisted that, "in the best interests of baseball," the Braves play him for at least two out of the three games. Hank hit his record-tying home run in his first at-bat, but he did not hit any homers in the second game, and he sat out the third, setting the stage for drama in Atlanta.

quieted but not disappeared. Everything was ready for him when he returned in the spring.

Nailing It, and Nailing It Again

The Braves' first game of the 1974 season was against the Reds, in Cincinnati. Hank was eager to hit a homer and put an end to some of the pressure. His first at-bat was in the first inning, against pitcher Jack Billingham. With a count of three balls and one strike, Hank had yet to swing his bat. On the fifth pitch, he took his first swing of the season, and he nailed it. As Hank circled the bases, his eyes became moist. For the first time, he felt as if he wasn't chasing anybody. He had made it. After more than 20 years of being told he couldn't, he had. He'd tied Babe Ruth's home run record. As he headed for home plate, his teammates were there, waiting to celebrate with him.

Hank didn't hit any more homers in the series with the Reds, and the next series was in Atlanta, against the Los Angeles Dodgers. It was the Braves' home opener, and Hank proudly watched his father throw out the first ball. Al Downing was on the mound, pitching for the Dodgers. Hank was careful and patient during his first at-bat. Then, in the fourth inning, he knew he had his shot.

The Dodgers were ahead, 3–1. Hank knew that Downing, not wanting to be the pitcher who served up a "softball" to the future home run king, would give him everything he had. His pitch was low, and Hank hit it squarely. Hank wasn't sure if he had used enough

A MOMENT ALONE

After Hank slammed his 715th home run out of the park, he was struck by just how difficult the whole chase had been. After a celebration with his family and friends at his house, Hank was able to take a moment to himself and reflect on his life and breaking the home run record:

"I went off downstairs to be by myself for a few minutes. When I was alone and the door was shut, I got down on my knees and closed my eyes and thanked God for pulling me through. At that moment, I knew what the past 25 years of my life had been all about ... I felt a deep sense of gratitude and a wonderful surge of liberation all at the same time."

Although hitting the epic home run had been overwhelming, Hank never forgot his quiet moment alone.

force to hit the ball out of the park. Normally, he never watched where the ball landed after hitting it—he was too busy rounding the bases. This time, however, Hank saw Dodger outfielder Bill Buckner leap against the fence. The ball was too high for Buckner, and it sailed past him, landing on the other side. By the time Hank touched first base, he knew he was the all-time home run king. He described rounding the bases as being like "running in a bubble."

As he rounded third and reached home, fans, teammates, and his family mobbed him and celebrated. His mother made it through the crowd and gave him a huge bear hug. The game was stopped, and Hank was given a special ceremony. At the microphone, Hank sighed with relief: "Thank God it's over."

THE HAMMER
AND BARRY BONDS

Many people still consider Hank Aaron to be baseball's home run king. Although his record has been surpassed by Barry Bonds of the San Francisco Giants, Bonds' bid sparked a lot of controversy in Major League Baseball and elsewhere in the world of sports and in society at large.

On August 7, 2007, playing the Washington Nationals in San Francisco, Bonds hit his 756th career home run. This hit surpassed Hank Aaron's final home run record and set the media on fire. But it wasn't positive attention. Bonds had previously been under investigation for steroid use, since 2003 and, Greg Anderson, Barry's trainer, was indicted by a grand jury and charged with supplying performance-enhancing steroids to athletes. People immediately began to wonder if Barry had been using steroids when there was no mandatory drug testing in the league. Eventually, he was charged with offenses in connection with a company with which Greg Anderson was associated.

Fans of any sport do not take kindly to the use of steroids, and baseball is no exception. It is seen as a type of cheating. People began to criticize Bonds, and he fell out of favor with most fans and the media. Although he eventually set the new home run mark at 762, the feeling in major-league ballparks was just not the same as it had been 33 years earlier. People were suspicious, not joyous, and many thought he didn't deserve the title. Commissioner Bud Selig, who is also Hank's longtime friend with ties to both the Milwaukee Braves and Brewers, was not in attendance to see Bonds' record-breaking hit.

Despite all of the controversy surrounding his prized record being broken, Hank was gracious and noble in his response to Bonds. He was not present for the record breaker, but he sent a prerecorded message that was played in the stadium during a ten-minute celebration: "I move over now and offer my best wishes to Barry and his family on this historical achievement. My hope today, as it was on that April evening in 1974, is that the achievement of this record will inspire others to chase their own dreams."

Bonds follows the path of the ball off his bat in a game against the Cincinnati Reds in San Francisco on August 25, 2006, nearly a year before his record-breaking 756th home run on August 7, 2007.

Chapter 6
Swinging Away at Fastballs and Bigotry

After hitting the home run heard around the world, Hank became one of America's most visible people. At first, folks saw him only as "the home run king," but he was much more than that. He was also a Gold Glove outfielder, the leader in all-time total bases and runs batted in, and a master baserunner. Hank had plans for his newfound fame. He wanted to keep giving back.

The Home Run King Moves On

Back in his secretary's office, Hank began to see just how much his record was affecting people. He began a scholarship program and raised a great deal of money from the 20,000 congratulatory telegrams that had arrived for

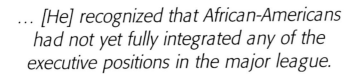

... [He] recognized that African-Americans had not yet fully integrated any of the executive positions in the major league.

him. Very quickly, Hank noticed people were always after autographs and pictures.

It was also at this time that Hank began to consider being a manager. He had no real desire to stop playing the game, but he recognized that African-Americans had not yet fully integrated any of the executive positions in the major league. Many agreed with him, and he recalled that Jackie Robinson had also spoken of the issue. He wasn't ready to move away from the game, so he kept his thoughts to himself.

Hank's new team would be the Milwaukee Brewers. Hank would finish his baseball career where it started. He was, in a sense, going home.

On the field during the weeks and months after breaking Ruth's record, Hank found himself somewhat lost. He was used to shooting after new records, and now he had achieved most of them. He knew the Braves were a good team, though not necessarily in contention for the World Series.

Hank considered retiring, but the thought of hitting the baseball a few more times was just too tempting for him. There was a wrinkle, however, to how much the decision to keep playing—and where—was actually in Hank's hands. The National League had assumed that 1974 would be his last season, so when the time came, they began showering him with farewell gifts. Seeing his loyal fans celebrate his career was one of the high points of Hank's life in baseball, yet he was fairly sure he didn't want to continue playing for the Braves in 1975. He opted instead for a front-office job, working as an executive with the Braves. Because of a previous contract as a spokesperson for other companies, however, Hank wouldn't be allowed to sell or endorse Braves' material. When the Braves realized this, they tried to give Hank a job at the bottom of the organization, but Hank knew he was not prepared to work his way up the corporate ladder.

At the same time, there was talk of a trade. The media wanted to know where he was headed, but Hank had no idea. He held a brief press conference, stating his last game would not be with the Braves. That was all he knew.

While away in Japan for a home run hitting contest, Hank received word that he had officially been traded. His new team would be the Milwaukee Brewers. Hank would finish his baseball career where it started. He was, in a sense, going home. He thought this was great news, and he was immediately eager to return to Milwaukee. The town, people, and baseball

The Return to
Where It All Began

Several famous baseball players have a history of returning to the cities where they started their major-league careers. Babe Ruth returned to Boston, where he had begun his career as a pitcher for the Red Sox, to play for the then-Boston Braves, and Willie Mays, whose career had begun with the New York Giants, returned to New York, playing for the Mets. When Hank Aaron returned to Milwaukee to play for the Brewers, he was ecstatic to "come home" to where his career had begun.

Milwaukee was just as excited to have Hank. For their 1975 season opener, the Brewers had 48,000 fans in County Stadium. This was the most the Brewers had ever drawn in their relatively short history as a major-league team. As he walked onto the field for his first game, Hank vividly remembered his teammates carrying him off of it after clinching the 1957 pennant. The Brewers fans, most of whom had followed Hank as a Milwaukee Brave only a few years back, serenaded him (to the tune of "Hello, Dolly!"), "Hello, Henry ... It's so nice to have you back where you belong."

Hank was also eager to work with his old friend, Bud Selig, who was then the owner of the team. Selig and Aaron respected each other, and Selig often sought out Hank's opinion about the team and how certain situations might best be handled. This relationship with his new team, fans, and owner—as well as the presence of one of his teammates from the old Braves, Del Crandall, as the manager of the Brewers—enhanced the feeling that Hank had indeed come home. To top it off, the All-Star game was being held in Milwaukee that year, and Hank was selected for the team for the 21st time in his career—this time as a representative of the American League. He may have been a 41-year-old hitter, but he was still a hitter. It would be Hank's final All-Star appearance.

Above, left to right: Two buttons celebrating Hank Aaron's return to Milwaukee in 1975–1976, including one showing Hank with a young Robin Yount at the beginning of what would also become a Hall of Fame career; and a commemorative bobblehead doll and box handed out at Miller Park during the Brewers' 2010 season.

"There's something magical about going back to where it all began—as if it will make everything begin all over again. I think the fans feel it too. Everybody wants to turn back the clock."

Hank Aaron, on returning to Milwaukee to finish out his career in the city where it began

Hank's plaque at the Baseball Hall of Fame in Cooperstown, New York.

felt like home. "I still loved Milwaukee, and unlike Atlanta, Milwaukee loved me," he recalled.

His first games with the Brewers seemed slower to him, and Hank realized that motivation was a big part of his success. Without a record to chase, he had to find new motivation within himself. He hit a two-run double in April, tying Ruth's all-time record for RBIs.

At the time of his trade, the Brewers played in the American League. (They moved to the National League at the start of the 1998 season.) The AL is different from the NL in at least one important way—the designated hitter rule, which allows teams to insert into the batting order a hitter who bats for the pitcher without the pitcher having to be taken out of the game. Pitchers play less frequently than other players because they tend to be weaker hitters. The designated hitter rule allows pitchers to stay in games without being taken out for pinch hitters, and it has also prolonged the careers of some players who might be less likely to be used at certain positions but can still be productive with their bats.

As a designated hitter in the AL, Hank found it difficult to pick up where he had left off. Playing for the Braves in the NL, Hank had learned the styles of every pitcher he ever encountered. But this was a new league for him, and he faced entirely new pitchers he knew nothing about. After a season, he found himself struggling with a .234 batting average.

In the 1976 season, Hank knew he was nearing the end of his professional career. He required glasses for reading, and his knees still

The covers for the Brewers' 1975 scorebooks, sold at all home games, were among several items made to highlight the return of Hank to the city and stadium where he began his career.

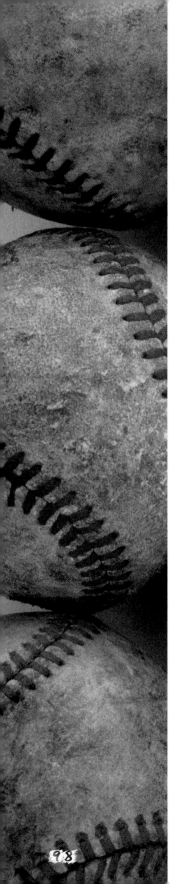

acted up, but he still had powerful moments that reminded fans of his earlier days. In June, he hit five home runs in a week. In July, he hit a home run in the tenth inning that gave the Brew Crew a sweep in a five-game series. The fans reacted with glee, and Hank was given a standing ovation. Now at 42, Hank enjoyed the feeling of every single home run and reveled in the sound of the fans chanting his name.

It was his 12,364th time at bat, which was more times than anybody had ever batted.

Hank's final home run took place in Milwaukee, against Dick Drago of the California Angels. It was his tenth that season and the 755th over his entire career. Soon after, it was time for Hank Aaron Day at Milwaukee County Stadium. It was also Hank's official retirement party. He was joined by his old friends and former ballplayers Félix Mantilla, Johnny Logan, Willie Mays, and more. Along with celebrating his career, Hank raised more money for his scholarship fund.

After his retirement party, Hank finished his final season. He was emotional before the last game even started, looking up with tears in his eyes at the fans who had come to see him off. It had been a physically and emotionally exhausting journey, but he cherished where his life had taken him.

He came up to bat during his 3,298th game, more games than anybody had played in Major League Baseball. It was his 12,364th time at bat, which was more times than anybody had ever batted. When he swung the bat, he had his 3,771st hit and 2,297th RBI. But, in that moment, Hank wasn't concerned with breaking records or hitting milestones. Hank thought,

"If I could come around to score, it would be my 2,175th run and would break my tie with Ruth, but when it came down to it, I didn't care very much about breaking another tie ... I sort of liked the idea of sharing something with the Babe."

Off the Field

After his final game, Hank knew his life would change. He was used to life as a ballplayer, so becoming someone who didn't play ball was a real adjustment for him. Hank was offered a job working for the Braves' farm system, being in charge of organizing teams and signing players.

In 1982, Hank was inducted by a nearly unanimous vote into the Baseball Hall of Fame. This made him feel that he had truly been accepted by the baseball community. The Hall of Fame induction was one of the most satisfying events of his life in baseball. He graciously spoke about his role in the game and thanked certain players, notably Jackie Robinson, for paving the way for other visible minorities in baseball. During the same year, he was named the Braves' director of playing

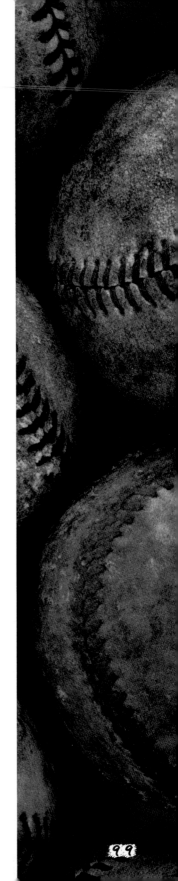

management and vice president.

As the Braves continued to improve race relations, acquire new teammates, and train players of many different backgrounds, Hank continued working with the team. In 1989, he became the senior vice president of the Braves. In 1999, on his 65th birthday, Major League Baseball announced its first major award in more than 30 years—the Hank Aaron Award, to be presented to two players: the best overall offensive player in each league.

2000 and Beyond

More than three decades after his last game, Hank is still a cornerstone of Major League Baseball. He has been called on to throw out the ceremonial pitch at two All-Star games and was presented with the Presidential Citizen's Medal by Bill Clinton. He also received the nation's highest civilian honor, the Presidential Medal of Freedom, from George W. Bush. To this day, he continues to work for civil rights and champions the movement to encourage African-Americans into the world of sports.

Hammerin' Hank: A Legacy

In the world of baseball, Hank Aaron is firmly etched into history. As former slugger and fellow Hall of Famer Reggie Jackson said, "You would need to hit 35 homers a year for 20 years and you still wouldn't reach Aaron's total." Hank's effect on baseball is clear. He dominated the record books, pushing himself to the limit. But his influence on the game came from more than a fleeting, blinding light of achievement.

Instead, his incredible numbers came from a game played consistently well over an entire generation. His achievement in baseball wasn't measured in MVP awards or even the home run record. He played patiently and tirelessly over 23 years, building himself into a rock-solid legend. Hank Aaron is a testament not only to determination and focus, but to endurance.

Over many years, he racked up more achievements than many thought were possible by one man. Even today, the man from Toulminville is the gold standard against which Major League Baseball hitters are judged.

Hank was about more than 6,856 total bases, 2,297 RBIs, and 755 home runs. Every time he picked up a bat, he was about right and wrong. His career was about social justice, and he fought every barrier he came up against. He showed up at the plate again and again, at a time and in a league where black people were still being told they had no right to be.

Playing for the Negro Leagues, he showed the world that he had talent and a right to dream. With the Sally League, he endured a lifetime of discrimination packed into one season for chasing his dreams, proving he and other African-Americans had a right to be there. And in Major League Baseball, for 23 seasons, he fought for civil rights the only way he knew how—he swung, and he swung hard. His sheer presence in baseball helped change the course of history, in Alabama, Florida, Milwaukee, Atlanta, and eventually the nation. Once he hit his last ball on the field, he worked for the same cause from another platform, focusing on minority relations in Major League Baseball.

A Lifetime Responsibility

When 18-year-old Hank stepped onto that train in Mobile to take him to his dreams, he had no idea how his life would turn out. After years being known as "Baseball's Greatest Hitter," Hank has never forgotten his roots or his cause. With his typical modesty and strength, he used what he had to make the world better.

Throughout his entire career, Hank saw that he had a big responsibility as a ballplayer. Being among the first African-Americans to integrate professional baseball, he knew he was doing important work. He wanted to set an example for black children everywhere; he wanted to give them a reason to try for what they wanted. In a world where African-Americans were made to feel less than they were, Hank made sure that every moment he spent on the field would give black children the strength to chase their dreams.

After surpassing the Babe and setting a new home run record with each one he hit, Hank could look back on his legacy. It was not so much about home runs as it was about hope. To every child watching him stride up to bat, Hank was hope personified. It was a responsibility he never took lightly:

"The way I see it, it's a great thing to be the man who hit the most home runs, but it's a greater thing to be the man who did the most with the home runs he hit. So as long as there's a chance that maybe I can hammer out a little justice now and then, or a little opportunity here and there, I intend to do as I always have—keep swinging."

Since Hank's retirement, statues of him grace the grounds of both Atlanta's Turner Field and Milwaukee's Miller Park. Both the Atlanta Braves and the Milwaukee Brewers have retired the number 44 he wore playing in both cities.

"If the home run record gives me more power to inspire children—and I know that it does—then the ordeal was worth every moment of sleep I lost and every hurt I felt from every hate letter."

Hank Aaron, talking about his legacy

44

Chronology

1934 Henry (Hank) Aaron is born in Mobile, Alabama, on February 5.

1947 Hank turns 13 a month before Jackie Robinson plays his first game for the Brooklyn Dodgers.

1950 Hank signs on to play for the Mobile Black Bears as a shortstop.

1952 Hank plays his first game with the Indianapolis Clowns. He is offered a contract with the Boston Braves. His signing bonus is a cardboard suitcase. He is assigned to the Eau Claire Bears of the Northern League, where he is named rookie of the year for the 1952 season.

1953 Hank Aaron, Félix Mantilla, and Horace Garner help integrate the Sally League when the now-Milwaukee Braves send them to their minor-league club in Jacksonville. He marries Barbara Lucas of Jacksonville. Playing for Caguas during winter ball in Puerto Rico, Hank becomes an outfielder.

1954 When Bobby Thomson breaks his ankle, Hank becomes the Braves' regular left fielder.

1955 Hank plays his first All-Star game; officially changes his uniform number from 5 to 44.

1957 Hank hits his 100th home run. He belts an 11th-inning homer against St. Louis, giving Milwaukee the National League pennant.

1958 Hank wins his first Gold Glove Award

1959 Hank hits three homers in one game, against the Giants.

1960 Hank hits his 200th homer in St. Louis.

1962 Hank's brother Tommie becomes a teammate on the Braves.

1963 Hank hits his 300th homer in Milwaukee.

1966 The Braves move to Atlanta. Soon after, he hits his 400th homer.

1968 Hank hits his 500th homer.

1970 Barbara and Hank divorce. Hank reaches 3,000th hit.

1971 Hank hits his 600th homer in Atlanta.

1973 Hank hits his 700th homer in Atlanta. He marries Billye Williams.

1974 Hank ties Babe Ruth's record with 714 homers in Cincinnati on the opening day of the season. Four days later, Hank hammers his 715th in Atlanta, setting a new major-league record. He is later traded to the Milwaukee Brewers, where he will finish his career in the city where it began.

1976 Hank hits his last home run, number 755, in Milwaukee. After two season with the Brewers, he retires. He has played 23 seasons in total.

1982 Hank is inducted into the Baseball Hall of Fame.

1987 The Atlanta Braves become the first baseball team with a Fair Share agreement. This includes a contract stipulating that minorities will get a fair share of opportunities, including professional services and executive positions.

1989 Hank is chosen as Senior Vice President and Assistant to the Braves' President.

1997 A new facility for the AA Mobile Bay Bears is built in Mobile, Alabama. It is named Hank Aaron Stadium.

1999 Major League Baseball establishes the Hank Aaron Award, given annually to the outstanding hitter in the National League and the American League.

2001 Hank is presented with the Presidential Citizens Medal by President Bill Clinton.

2002 Hank receives the Presidential Medal of Freedom from President George W. Bush.

2007 The Atlanta Braves are sold, with Hank being retained to continue to work with the team. Baseball Commissioner Bug Selig also announces that Hank will work with Major League Baseball to develop programs to help encourage minorities into the game.

Glossary

acclimate To become accustomed, or used, to a new environment

barnstorming Traveling to various locations to play exhibition games with other teams

charismatic Having personal appeal, charm, or energy that attracts others

color line The denying of rights, facilities, or opportunities to one group on the basis of skin color

confiscate To seize or take something away deemed harmful or illegal by an authority

contending Performing at a level of play which is likely to lead a team to championship playoffs

defeatist Having an attitude that surrenders or resigns easily

desegregate To eliminate the segregation, or separation, of people, usually on the basis of race

designated hitter In the American League, a regular position in the batting order for a player who hits for the pitcher in the pitcher's spot in the order. Rather than being substituted for and having to leave the game, the pitcher is allowed to remain in the game to pitch to the opposing team. The designated hitter is used on offense only and does not take the field and play defense.

discrimination The unfair treatment of a person or group based on prejudice

doubleheader A sporting event in which teams play two games in a row at the same place

eleventh hour The last possible moment

fast-pitch softball A form of baseball that uses a larger ball and underhand pitching

hitting for average When a player achieves a high batting average

hitting safely When a batter reaches a base without being tagged or an error being committed

impede To be an obstacle, or get in the way of something

indict To accuse formally of a crime.

integrated When an organization accepts people, usually of different races, as equal and full members.

Major League Baseball (MLB) The highest level of professional baseball in North America. Within the major leagues are two separate leagues—the National League and the American League.

minor leagues Groupings of professional teams—most of them affiliated with teams in the major leagues—that are made up of players who have less experience than it takes to reach the majors. In baseball, players are assigned to minor-league teams to gain experience and work on developing skills in hitting, pitching, and fielding.

NAACP (National Association for the Advancement of Colored People) A civil rights organization. Its mission is to ensure equality for all people and to eliminate racial hatred and discrimination.

Negro Leagues Professional baseball leagues created for African-Americans when MLB was still segregated

notorious Well known for a particularly negative trait

pennant The championship award given to the best team in a baseball league. In Major League Baseball, the pennant winners from the American League and the National League play one another in the World Series.

perfect game When a pitcher pitches a "no-hitter" where no batters from the opposing team make it to a base

pickup games In sports, games that are not part of a regularly scheduled competition or played in a conventional arena or stadium

prejudice A preconceived belief, opinion, or judgment toward a person or group often based on their race or ethnicity

relentless Being persistent and not stopping

rookie An inexperienced athlete playing his or her first season with a sports team

scout In sports, a person who watches and reports on specific players. Scouts often recommend new talent for recruitment.

segregation To separate or divide into groups, often on the basis of race. Racial segregation was common in early professional baseball.

showboating Showing off, looking for attention

steroid A class of chemicals that promotes the growth of muscle. In sports, it's use is often illegal

sweep To win every game in a series

Triple Crown An award given to a batter who leads the league in home runs, runs batted in, and batting average

unanimous Showing complete agreement, often by a vote

World Series The championship series of Major League Baseball that is held yearly between the winners of the National and American League pennants. It is often known as the "Fall Classic" because it takes place in October.

Further Information

Books

Aaron, Hank, and Lonnie Wheeler. *I Had A Hammer: The Hank Aaron Story.*
Toronto, ON: HarperCollins, 2007.

Bryant, Howard. *The Last Hero: A Life of Henry Aaron.*
New York: Pantheon, 2010.

Golenbock, Peter. *Hank Aaron: Brave In Every Way.*
New York: Harcourt, 2001.

Nelson, Kadir. *We Are the Ship: The Story of Negro League Baseball.*
New York: Jump at the Sun, 2008.

Poolos, J. *Hank Aaron* (Baseball Superstars).
New York: Checkmark Books, 2008.

Vascellaro, Charlie. *Hank Aaron: A Biography* (Baseball's All-Time Greatest
Hitters) Westport, CT: Greenwood, 2005.

Web sites

http://755homeruns.com/
Part of the *Baseball Almanac,* this site explores Hank Aaron's life and
accomplishments with links to timelines, player on player statistics and
home run archive.

www.sportingnews.com/archives/aaron/
This site is an online scrapbook chronicling Hank's career. Included are links
to a photo gallery, audio interviews, home run breakdowns, and career
statistics. There is also a copy of Hank's Baseball Register from 1953.

http://www.life.com/image/81500633/in-gallery/24671
As a young and unknown player, Hank often looked to his teammates for support and guidance. This photography site looks back on the influence other players have had on Hank's career, coupled with his own exclusive commentary.

www.negroleaguebaseball.com/
The official "Online Home of Negro League Baseball History," this website features a wide range of fascinating articles, stories, photographs, and other items that convey the incredible vitality of America's "other major leagues," as well as the history and culture of the society at large.

www.milwaukeebraves.info/
Featuring a host of photographs, stories, and memorabilia, this site is part shrine, part historical archive, and part blog dedicated to preserving the memory of the team that began the modern movement of franchises when it left Boston for Milwaukee in 1953. It also chronicles the team's love affair with the city that took it into its hearts for 13 "glorious" years, all of them winning seasons, a mark that no other franchise can claim.

http://atlanta.braves.mlb.com/index.jsp?c_id=atl
This is the official site of the Atlanta Braves, where baseball first ventured into the South as a venue for its major leagues. This is the team for which Hank Aaron played for nine seasons, including 1974, the year in which he broke Babe Ruth's all-time home run record.

http://milwaukee.brewers.mlb.com/index.jsp?c_id=mil
This is the official site of the Milwaukee Brewers, the American League team that brought Hank Aaron "home" for the final two seasons of his career, renewing the bond between a city and its baseball hero and bringing credibility to a franchise that was trying to fill the big shoes left behind when the Braves left for Atlanta.

Video

Hank Aaron: Chasing the Dream (VHS). Turner Home Entertainment, 1996.

Index

Index

About the Author

Jessica Morrison is a writer, educator, and sculptor. She attended the University of Guelph for a degree in Zoology and a Masters of Science degree. The author of numerous nonfiction books for children, she is constantly on the lookout for people and places with a story to tell. She has also written about Wayne Gretzky for Crabtree Publishing and is currently writing her first novel.